TUNISIAN CROCHET

TUNISIAN CROCHET

Gorgeous designs to wear for all seasons

HELLE KAMPP MATHORNE

SEARCH PRESS

First published in Great Britain in 2025 by
Search Press Limited
Wellwood, North Farm Road,
Tunbridge Wells, Kent TN2 3DR

Originally published as *Tunesisk hækling til alle årstider*
© Turbine 2023

English translation by Burravoe Translation Services

Photos: Oliver Rosendal / VINIA Media
Image retouching: Mathias Vilhelmsen / VINIA Media
Specialist editing: Rachel Søgaard
Graphic design: Karin Hald

ISBN: 978-1-80092-240-2
ebook ISBN: 978-1-80093-227-2

Suppliers
If you have difficulty in obtaining any of the materials and equipment mentioned in this
book, then please visit the Search Press website for details of suppliers:
www.searchpress.com

Bookmarked Hub
For further ideas and inspiration, and to join our free online community, visit
www.bookmarkedhub.com

You are invited to visit the author's
Website: www.kampp-design.dk
Instagram: @kamppdesign

Contents

Introduction

This book has been many years in the making. My first hopes and dreams of creating an inspiring book about this technique began 30 years ago and has only increased since then. The technique comes from North Africa and Central Asia (including Afghanistan and the Middle East), and is known as both Tunisian and Afghan crochet. I am deeply fascinated with this technique, which is a combination of knitting and crochet and creates a broad spectrum of fabric, from a dense, textured look to one that is lighter and airier.

I remember that when I first came across this technique I thought, 'Wow, if you can bring these two worlds – knitting and crochet – together, there will be undreamt opportunities for new designs.'

The subtitle, 'gorgeous designs to wear for all seasons' can be understood in several ways – partly the seasons in the form of spring, summer, autumn, winter and their colours, but also seasons in connection with a woman's age and the female form. From the beginning my wish was to unite these two ideas.

Exploring and experimenting with techniques has resulted in 17 designs that envelop the seasons in a wonderful harmony of colours, shapes, patterns and lovely yarns. All this is emphasized by the beautiful women who wear the pieces in the book.

Once all the main photos were taken at the photoshoot, there was a free-for-all. The women who wore my designs took turns in wearing the various blouses, sweaters and jackets, even though the sizes were not intended for them. That created a magical universe of new possibilities, and these inspiring additional photos also appear in the book.

Various techniques are presented at the end of the book. Videos of some of the more unusual techniques can be found on my website: www.kampp-design.dk

Designing the projects and writing this book has been a fairytale journey and it is only the start of a long voyage with new perspectives and opportunities.

I hope that with this book I will be able to contribute to many warm, pleasant and inspiring moments.

Happy crocheting!

Abbreviations

All patterns are written using US crochet terms. Conversions to UK terms are shown in the table opposite.

alt = alternate
ch = chain
ch row = chain row
dec = decrease
dc = double crochet (*UK treble crochet*)
dwht = double wheat stitch
FP = forward pass
inc = increase
k = knit
k2tog = knit 2 stitches together
k3tog = knit 3 stitches together
p = purl
p2tog tbl = purl 2 stitches together through back loop
R = return stitch
R3tog = work 3 stitches together on the return pass
rep = repeat
RP = return pass

sc = single crochet (*UK double crochet*)
sl = slip
st(s) = stitch(es)
tbl = through the back loop
Tks = Tunisian knit stitch
T-cross = Tunisian crossed stitch
Tdc = Tunisian double crochet (*UK Tunisian treble crochet*)
tog = together
Tps = Tunisian purl stitch
T-rib = Tunisian rib stitch
Tss = Tunisian simple stitch
wht = wheat stitch
wyib = with yarn in back
wyif = with yarn in front
yo = yarn over (wrap yarn around hook)

Conversion chart

US	UK
double crochet (dc)	treble crochet (tr)
half double crochet (hdc)	half treble crochet (htr)
single crochet (sc)	double crochet (dc)
skip	miss
slip stitch (sl st/ss)	slip stitch (sl st/ss)

Measuring a Tunisian swatch

Crochet a swatch before you start work. The hook size given in the patterns is always just a guideline, because we do not all produce the same gauge (tension) when we crochet. Some people crochet tightly and others loosely, so I cannot emphasize the importance of making a swatch too strongly.

Tunisian crochet is not particularly elastic, and not at all if the yarn used is not stretchy.

If the work is too tight, it cannot be worn in the same way as a knitted top, which would be more flexible.

Crochet a swatch that is at least four stitches larger at each side and at least two forward and return rows larger at the top and bottom, so you can easily measure 4 x 4in (10 x 10cm) over the swatch.

Use either a tape measure and pins or a calculator/counting frame to check the gauge (tension) (see opposite).

Horizontally you count the vertical bars and vertically you count the rows (1 row = 1 forward and return pass).

KNITTING CALCULATOR AND SWATCH RULER METHOD

Here you can see how to count stitches/vertical bars and rows in the 4 x 4in (10 x 10cm) opening of the frame.

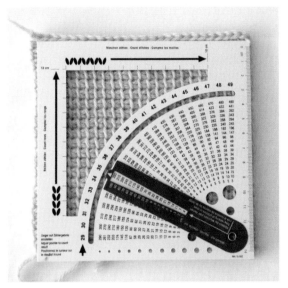

1. **Horizontally:** count the number of vertical bars within the frame.

2. **Vertically:** count the number of rows within the frame. A row consists of a forward and return pass.

TAPE MEASURE AND PINS METHOD

Measure 4in (10cm) in each direction and insert pins.

Determine the gauge (tension) by counting stitches/vertical bars and rows between the pins as follows:

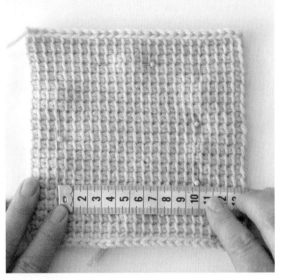

1. **Horizontally:** count the number of stitches/vertical bars between the pins.

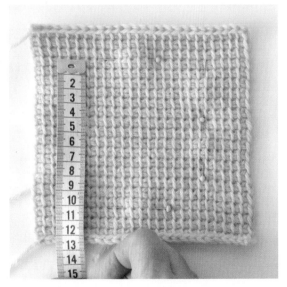

2. **Vertically:** count the number of rows between the pins. A row consists of a forward and return pass.

Spring

WINTER ACONITE

V-neck cardigan with knitted front band

SIZES
US (4:6:8:10:12:14)/UK (8:10:12:14:16:18)

FINISHED MEASUREMENTS
Bust
39¾(43:44:46:48:50)in /
101(109:112:117:122:127)cm
Hips
41¾(45:46:47¾:50:52)in /
106(114:117:121:127:132)cm
Length
26½(26½:26½:27¼:27¼:27¼)in /
67(67:67:69:69:69)cm

MATERIALS
Yarn
4(4:5:5:5:6) balls of Isager Yarn Alpaca 1
(lace/2-ply) 100% alpaca in shade 40;
1¾oz/50g/438yd/400m
8(8:9:9:9:10) balls of Isager Silk
Mohair (lace/2-ply) 75% super kid mohair,
25% silk in shade 59; 1oz/25g/232yd/212m
Tunisian crochet hook (suggested)
7mm (US 10½/11, UK 2), 16in (40cm) cable
Circular knitting needle
4mm (US 6, UK 8), 32in (80cm) cable
Stitch markers
2
Buttons
7 (not too heavy), ¾in (20mm) diameter

GAUGE (TENSION)
17 sts x 12 rows (FP and RP) = 4 x 4in
(10 x 10cm) in pattern using 1 strand of
each yarn and 7mm (US 10½/11, UK 2)
Tunisian crochet hook

SPECIAL TECHNIQUES
End stitch at left edge in 1 vertical bar
(see Techniques, page 136)
**Decreasing at both sides on the
return pass** (see Techniques, page 154)
Increasing in back vertical bar
(see Techniques, page 152)
**Binding (casting) off for armhole with
slip stitch, both sides** (see Techniques,
page 147)
**Binding (casting) off for shoulder slope,
left side** (see Techniques, page 144)
**Binding (casting) off for shoulder slope,
right side** (see Techniques, page 146)

BUTTONHOLE WITH 2 YARN OVERS:
Step 1 (right side): work to where the
buttonhole is to be, k2tog (or p2tog, as fits
the pattern), yo twice, k2togtbl (or p2tog,
as fits the pattern).
Step 2 (wrong side): work to the 2 yo and
work as k1, p1 (or p1, k1, as fits the pattern).

Instructions

The front, back and sleeves are worked in rows.

BACK

Using 7mm (US 10½/11, UK 2) Tunisian crochet hook and one strand of each yarn, 91(95:99:103:109:113) ch.

FP 1: start in the second ch from the hook and pick up sts in the back loops of the ch row until you have a total of 91(95:99:103:109:113) sts on the hook.

RP 1: work in shell rib (see chart) as follows: 1 end st, 7(6:8:4:4:6) R, 1 ch, R3tog, 1 ch, *3 R, 1 ch, R3tog, 1 ch, rep from * to last 7(6:8:4:4:6) sts before end st, 7(6:8:4:4:6) R, 1 end st.

FP 2: 1 end st, 7(6:8:4:4:6) Tps, 1 Tss round the ch sp, 1 Tss in the top of the R3tog, 1 Tss round ch sp, *3 Tps, 1 Tss round ch sp, 1 Tss in the top of the R3tog, 1 Tss round ch sp*, rep from * to last 7(6:8:4:4:6) sts before end st, 7(6:8:4:4:6) Tps, 1 end st.

RP 1 and FP 2 make up pattern.

Continue in pattern without shaping, until work measures 4in (10cm).

Dec 1 st for hips at each side of next RP.

Then dec 1 st at each side on foll fourth RP four times (81(85:89:93:99:103) sts).

Work 3 FP and RP without shaping.

Inc 1 st at each side on next FP.

Then inc 1 st at each side on foll sixth FP twice (87(91:95:99:105:109) sts).

SHELL RIB CHART

Multiple of 6 sts + 3.

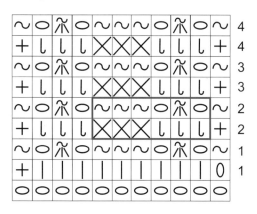

To see a video of the shell being worked, please visit www.kampp-design.dk and search for 'Muslingerib' ('shell rib' in Danish).

$\sim$ = RP

| = FP

X = Tps

| = Tss

⋏ = R3tog

L = Tss round ch sp or in top of R3tog

+ = end st

○ = ch

☐ = pattern repeat

∼ = return st

Continue without shaping until work measures 16¼(16¼:16¼:16¼:16½:15¾)in / 41.5(41.5:41:41.5:42:40)cm.

Bind (cast) off 4(5:5:4:5:5) sts for the armhole at each side of the next FP as follows:

Work sl st over the first 4(5:5:4:5:5) sts, work to the last 4(5:5:4:5:5) sts and work sl st over these. Break off the yarn. Join the yarn to the remaining sts and work the RP in pattern.

Then dec at each side immediately before the end stitch as follows:

Sizes US 4, 6 and 8 (UK 8, 10 and 12): dec 1 st on foll 6(9:8:−:−:−) RP, then foll 2(−:1:−:−:−) alt RP.

Size US 10 (UK 14): dec 2 sts on foll two alt RP, then dec 1 st on foll six alt RP, and then on next alt RP.

Sizes US 12 and 14 (UK 16 and 18): dec 2 sts on foll −(−:−:−:3:2) RP, then dec 1 st foll −(−:−:−:5:8) RP, and then on next alt RP. There are 63(63:67:69:71:73) sts remaining.

Continue without shaping, until work measures 24¾(24¾:24¾:25½: 25½:25½)in / 63(63:63:65:65:65)cm.

Place a marker on each side of the middle 13(13:13:15:15:15) sts. Work to the first marker, work sl st over the next 13(13:13:15:15:15) sts and work to end of FP. Complete the shoulder at the left end of the hook first. Bind (cast) off 5(5:5:5:5:6) sts at the neck edge on foll 1(2:2:1:2:1) FP, and then 4(−:−:4:−:5) sts on foll 1(−:−:1:−:1) FP. Bind (cast) off 8(7:9:9:9:9) sts for the shoulder slope from left to right on foll 2(1:1:2:2:2) FP, then bind (cast) off −(8:8:−:−:−) sts on foll −(1:1:−:−:−) FP. Bind (cast) off with sl st over the remaining sts.

Work the shoulder at the right end of the hook in the same way, binding (casting) off for the shoulder slope from right to left.

LEFT FRONT

Using a 7mm (US 10½/11, UK 2) Tunisian crochet hook and 1 strand of each yarn, 42(47:47:49:51:53) ch.

FP 1: start in the second ch from the hook and pick up sts in the back loops of the ch row until you have a total of 42(47:47:49:51:53) sts on the hook.

RP 1: work in pattern as follows: 1 end st, 1 ch, R3tog, 1 ch, *3 R, 1 ch, R3tog, 1 ch, rep from * to last 7(6:6:2:4:6) sts before end st, 7(6:6:2:4:6) R.

FP 2: 1 end st, 7(6:6:2:4:6) Tps, 1 Tss round the ch sp, 1 Tss in the top of the R3Tog, 1 Tss round ch sp, *3 Tps, 1 Tss round the ch sp, 1 Tss in the top of the R3Tog, 1 Tss round ch sp, rep from * to the last st, 1 end st.

Continue without shaping in pattern, until work measures 4in (10cm).

Dec 1 st for the hip at the right side immediately before the end st on next RP. Then dec 1 st on foll fourth RP four times (37(42:42:44:46:48) sts).

Work 3 FP and RP without shaping.

Inc 1 st at the right side immediately before the end st on next FP.

Then inc 1 st on foll sixth FP twice (40(45:45:47:49:51) sts).

Continue without shaping, until work measures 16½(16⅜:16⅜:16⅜:16¼:15¾)in / 42(41.5:41.5:41.5:41:40)cm.

Bind (cast) off 3(5:5:5:6:4) sts for armhole at right side on next FP by working sl st over the first 3(5:5:5:6:4) sts.

Then dec immediately before the end st at the armhole side as follows:

Sizes US 4, 6 and 8 (UK 8, 10 and 12): dec 1 st on foll RP 5(8:7:−:−:−) times and 1(−:1:−:−:−) st on foll alt RP 4(−:1:−:−:−) times.

Sizes US 10, 12 and 14 (UK 14, 16 and 18): dec 2 sts on foll RP −(−:−:2:1:4) times, 1 st on foll RP −(−:−:6:7:6) times and 1 st on foll alt RP −(−:−:1:1:−) times.

There are 28(32:32:31:33:33) sts remaining. Continue without further shaping at the armhole side.

At the same time when work measures 19(18:18¼:18¾:18¾:18¾)in / 48(46:46.5:47.5:47.5:47.5)cm, begin decreasing for the V-neck at the left side. Dec by working sts 4 and 5 tog (excluding end st) on the RP and working the Tps on the next FP, to make a shell border around the neck. Dec 1 st on foll 5(7:7:3:4:5) RP. Then dec 1 st on foll 8(9:8:11:11:10) alt RP (15(16:17:17:18:18) sts).

At the same time when work measures 25½(25½:25½:26:26:26½)in / 65(65:65:66:66:67)cm, bind (cast) off for the shoulder slope from right to left 8(8:9:9:9:9) sts on foll 1(2:1:1:2:2) FP, and then 7(–:8:8:–:–) sts on foll 1(–:1:1:–:–) FP.

RIGHT FRONT

Work as for left front, but reversing shapings, binding (casting) off for the shoulder slope from left to right.
Bind (cast) off the shoulder by working sl st over all sts.

SLEEVES

Using one strand of each yarn and 7mm (US 10½/11, UK 2) crochet hook, 41(43:43:45:45:47) ch.

FP 1: start in the second ch from the hook and pick up sts in the back loops of the ch row until you have a total of 41(43:43:45:45:47) sts on the hook.

RP 1: work in pattern as follows: 1 end st, 3(4:4:2:2:3) R, 1 ch, R3tog, 1 ch, *3 R, 1 ch, R3tog, 1 ch, rep from * to last 3(4:4:2:2:3) sts before end st, and work 3(4:4:2:2:3) R, 1 end st.

Work 1 FP and RP without shaping.
Then inc at each side as follows: inc 1 st each side on foll 3rd(3rd:3rd:3rd:3rd:2nd) FP 5(5:12:13:16:4) times,then on foll 4th(4th:4th:4th:2nd:3rd) FP 8(8:3:2:1:14) times, and then inc 1(1:1:1:–:–) st on foll 2nd(2nd:2nd:2nd:–:–) FP 1(1:1:1:–:–) times (69(71:75:77:79:83) sts).

Continue without shaping, until work measures 16¼(16¼:16½:16½:16½:16½)in / 41.5(41.5:42:42:42:42)cm.
Bind (cast) off 4(4:5:4:4:4) sts for top of sleeve at each side on next FP as follows: work sl st over the first 4(4:5:4:4:4) sts, work to the last 4(4:5:4:4:4) sts and work sl st over these. Break off the yarn. Join the yarn to the remaining sts and work back in pattern.

N.B.: note that you decrease on both FP and RP in the following section, depending on the size.
Dec at each side immediately before the end st as follows:

Size US 4 (UK 8): dec 2 sts twice on foll RP, dec 3 sts once on foll third RP, dec 1 st twice on foll alt RP, dec 1 st three times on foll RP, dec 1 st once on foll alt RP, dec 1 st once and 2 sts three times on foll FP.

Size US 6 (UK 10): dec 2 sts three times and 1 st once on foll alt RP, dec 1 st six times on foll RP, dec 1 st once on fo
ll third RP, dec 3 sts twice on foll FP.

Size US 8 (UK 12): dec 3 sts once on alt RP, dec 2 sts twice and 1 st once on foll alt RP, dec 1 st six times on foll RP, dec 2 sts once on foll third RP, dec 2 sts once on foll alt RP, dec 3 sts once on foll FP.

Size US 10 (UK 14): dec 3 sts twice on foll alt RP, dec 2 sts once on foll alt RP, dec 1 st four times on foll alt RP, dec 1 st twice on foll RP, dec 1 st once on foll alt RP, dec 3 sts once and 4 sts once on foll FP.

Size US 12 (UK 16): dec 3 sts twice on foll alt RP, dec 2 sts once on alt RP, dec 1 st three times on foll alt RP, dec 1 st three times on foll RP, dec 1 st once, dec 2 sts once on alt RP and 3 sts once on foll alt RP, dec 3 sts once on foll FP.

Size US 14 (UK 18): dec 2 sts three times on foll RP, dec 1 st twice on foll alt FP, dec 1 st seven times on foll RP, dec 1 st once on foll alt RP, dec 2 sts once on foll alt RP, dec 3 sts once on foll alt RP, dec 3 sts once on foll FP. There are 21(23:23:25:25:27) sts remaining. Bind (cast) off with sl st.

FINISHING

Join the side, shoulder and sleeve seams with backstitch with wrong sides together. Sew the sleeves into the armholes with backstitch with wrong sides together.

FRONT BAND

Using a 4mm (US 6, UK 8) circular knitting needle pick up and knit sts with the right side facing as follows: start at the bottom of the right front, k1 in the end st, yo, *k1, yo, rep from * along right front and right side of the neck, k1 in each st and each ch along the back neck, continue along the left side of the neck and the left front as for the right front until the last row. Make sure that the number of sts is the same along both fronts.

Work 3 rows in k1, p1 rib. Make buttonholes over the next 2 rows (See **SPECIAL TECHNIQUES**, buttonhole with 2 yarn overs, page 15) as follows:

Work 4 sts, *work a buttonhole, work 14 sts*, rep from * to * a further five times, work a buttonhole, work to end of row.

Work a further 4 rows in rib.

Bind (cast) off using Italian bind- (cast-) off (see Techniques, page 170).

Weave in all ends.

Sew on buttons using one strand of each yarn.

BUD

Crochet skirt with knitted rib hem

SIZES
US 4(6:8:10:12)/UK 8(10:12:14:16)

FINISHED MEASUREMENTS
Waist
33(35½:37¾:40¼:42½)in /
84(90:96:102:108)cm
Hips
36¼(38½:41:43¼:45¾)in /
92(98:104:110:116)cm
Length
18(18:19:19¾:19¾)in / 46(46:48:50:50)cm

MATERIALS
Yarn
6(6:7:7:8) balls of Filcolana Pernilla (light
fingering/3-ply) 100% Peruvian Highland
wool in 822 Willow; 1¾oz/50g/192yd/175m
Tunisian crochet hook (suggested)
6mm (US 10, UK 4) double-ended
6mm (US 10, UK 4) single-ended hook
with cable
Circular knitting needle
4mm (US 6, UK 8), 32in (80cm) cable
5mm (US 8, UK 6), 32in (80cm) cable
Double-pointed knitting needles
4mm (US 6, UK 8)

Scrap yarn
39¼in (1m) of a contrasting colour,
preferably cotton or similar
Stitch markers
Approx. 27
Elastic
39¼in (1m), max. ⅝in (1.5cm) wide
Sewing necessities
Pins and 1 safety pin

GAUGE (TENSION)
20 sts x 16 rows (FP and RP) = 4 x 4in
(10 x 10cm) in rib pattern using 6mm
(US 10, UK 4) Tunisian crochet hook

SPECIAL TECHNIQUES
Italian cast-on (see Techniques, page 169)
Working in rounds (see Techniques,
page 164)
Decreasing at both sides on return pass
(see Techniques, page 154)
Increasing in back vertical bar
(see Techniques, page 152)
**Binding (casting) off/decreasing on
forward pass** (see Techniques, page 143)
Binding (casting) off with slip stitch in rib
(see Techniques, page 142)

RIB PATTERN CHART

Even number of sts over 14 rounds.

FP 1: *1 Tps, 1 Tss, rep from * to end of round.

RP 1–14: work in return st.

FP 2: *1 Tps, 1 Tss, rep from * to end of round.

FP 3: *1 Tss, 1 Tps, rep from * to end of round.

FP 4: *1 Tss, 1 Tps, rep from * to end of round.

FP 5: *1 Tps, 1 Tss, rep from * to end of round.

FP 6: *1 Tps, 1 Tss, rep from * to end of round.

FP 7: *1 Tps, 1 Tss, rep from * to end of round.

FP 8: *1 Tss, 1 Tps, rep from * to end of round.

FP 9: *1 Tss, 1 Tps, rep from * to end of round.

FP 10: *1 Tps, 1 Tss, rep from * to end of round.

FP 11: *1 Tps, 1 Tss, rep from * to end of round.

FP 12: *1 Tss, 1 Tps, rep from * to end of round.

FP 13: *1 Tss, 1 Tps, rep from * to end of round.

FP 14: *1 Tss, 1 Tps, rep from * to end of round.

Rep rounds 1–14 over the entire garment. The rib pattern is shown in the chart.

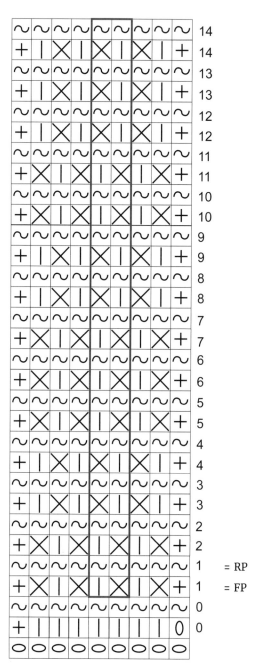

= RP

= FP

☒ = Tps   ☐ = end st

❘ = Tss   ⬭ = ch

∼ = return st   ☐ = pattern repeat

Instructions

The skirt is worked in rounds from the bottom up.

RIB HEM

The rib hem is worked with yarn held double. Using a 4mm (US 6, UK 8) circular needle and scrap yarn held double, cast on 170(182:194:206:218) sts using Italian cast-on.

On round 1, divide the sts so you can work (k2, p2). This round is a bit special, as some of the stitches are twisted around one another, as follows:

Round 1: knit the end st and first st tog, *sl2 wyib, slip sts individually back onto the left needle, k1, p2, k1*, rep from * to * until last 4 sts, sl2 wyib, slip sts individually back onto the left needle, k1, p1, p2togtbl.

Place a marker at the start of the round. There are 168(180:192:204:216) sts remaining on the circular needle.

Work 4 rounds in pattern as set.

SKIRT

Change to the 6mm (US 10, UK 4) double-ended Tunisian crochet hook and single yarn. Do not break the yarn.

Use one strand for the FP and the other for the RP.

Divide the work into front and back by placing a marker at each side. The first marker shows the start of the round. Place the second marker after 84(90:96:102:108) sts.

Work in rounds as follows:

First round (Round 0 on chart): using the double-ended hook and one strand of yarn, pick up as many sts as possible (knitting them onto the crochet hook). Turn the work, and using the other strand of yarn work a normal RP. When about 5 sts remain on the hook, turn the work again and pick up more sts with the first strand of yarn. Continue in this way until you've worked all the way around.

Second round (Round 1 on chart): this is the first pattern FP and RP of the rib pattern. Continue following the written pattern or the chart.

Work without shaping until work measures 3½(3½:4¼:5:5)in / 8.5(8.5:10.5: 12.5:12.5)cm.

N.B.: If you would like the skirt a little longer, you can increase the length here.

All sizes

In the following steps you dec and inc at each side of the front and back. Place a marker between the increases and decreases at each side of the front and back as the work grows.

Next round: inc 1 st at each side of both markers. Then inc 1 st at each side of both markers on foll tenth FP once, and then inc 1 st at each side of both markers on foll ninth FP twice (184(196:208:220:232) sts). Adapt the increases into the pattern.

The work now measures 10¼(10¼:11:11¾: 11¾)in / 26(26:28:30:30)cm.

Work 10 rounds without shaping.

Dec 1 st for the waist at each side of the front and back on the RP.

Dec 1 st each side of marker on next fifth RP, then on foll seventh RP twice (168(180:192:204:216) sts).

The last round is a RP. Break off the yarn.

Change to a 6mm (US 10, UK 4) Tunisian crochet hook with cable and work in rows. Start at the left side of the front, with the right side facing you. Count 12(12:12:14:14) sts in from the side marker towards the centre front.

The 12th(12th:12th:14th:14th) st is the first st of the FP. Work in pattern to the opposite side of the front, finish the row 12(12:12:14:14) sts in from the side marker and work back.

On the next FP, bind (cast) off 6(6:6:7:7) sts at each side.

Work back.

Break off the yarn.

TOP EDGE

Start at one side of the skirt.

Work 1 round sl st in pattern in the vertical bar.

Knitted I-cord edging

Using 4mm (US 6, UK 8) DPN, cast on 3 sts. *Pick up one st from the sl st row, k2, k2togtbl, slide stitches to the other end of the DPN, rep from *, bringing the yarn around the back to continue the I-cord. Work I-cord edging around entire top of skirt (168(180:192:204:216) sts). Bind off the last 3 sts.

FINISHING

Graft the two ends of the I-cord edging together on the right side.

Sew up the little opening in the rib border in the same way.

Turn wrong side out. Weave in the ends.

Creating the elastic casing

Turn the work right side out and fold the I-cord edging down on to the right side of the skirt so the slip stitch row is visible. Using a 4mm (US 6, UK 8) circular knitting needle and one strand of yarn, start at one side and pick up sts from the back loops of the sl st row. These sts will form the elastic casing.

Knit 6 rounds and bind (cast) off loosely as follows:

k2, *return 2 sts to the left needle, k2tog, k1, rep from * to end of round.

Before breaking off the yarn, pull extra yarn from the ball twice the circumference of the waist. Break off the yarn and pull the end through the last st.

Fold the I-cord edging back in place and fold the casing wrong sides together with the skirt.

Sew in place on the skirt with whip st, leaving a little opening.

Measure the elastic to the waist size plus 1½in (4cm) and pull it through the casing, using the safety pin to help guide it.

Sew the elastic together in a ring with 1½in (4cm) overlap. Sew up the little opening with whip st.

ANEMONE

V-neck sweater with ribbing

SIZES
US 4(6:8:10:12:14)/UK 8(10:12:14:16:18)

FINISHED MEASUREMENTS
Bust
42¼(43¾:45¾:47¼:50:51½)in /
107(111:116:120:127:131)cm
Length
24¼(24½:24¾:25¼:25½:25¾)in /
61.5(62.5:63:64:64.5:65.5)cm

MATERIALS
Yarn
6(6:7:7:8:8) balls of Filcolana Saga
(light fingering/3-ply) 100% wool in
301 Hoarfrost; 1¾oz/50g/328yd/300m
11(11:12:12:14:14) balls of Filcolana Alva
(lace/2-ply) 100% alpaca in 281 Rimefrost;
1oz/25g/192yd/175m
Tunisian crochet hook (suggested)
7mm (US 10½/11, UK 2) double-ended
7mm (US 10½/11, UK 2) single-ended with
16in (40cm) cable
Standard crochet hook
5mm (US 8, UK 6)
Circular knitting needle
4mm (US 6, UK 8), 32in (80cm) cable if you
knit with magic loop
Stitch markers
10

GAUGE (TENSION)
18 sts x 14 rows (FP and RP) = 4 x 4in
(10 x 10cm) in pattern using one strand
of each yarn and 7mm (US 10½/11, UK 2)
crochet hook

SPECIAL TECHNIQUES
End stitch at left edge in 2 vertical bars
(see Techniques, page 138)
Working in rounds (see Techniques,
page 164)
Decreasing at both sides on return pass
(see Techniques, page 154)
Increasing in back vertical bar
(see Techniques, page 152)
Raglan increase in back vertical bar
(see Techniques, page 148)
Italian bind- (cast-) off (see Techniques,
page 170)

MOSS STITCH
Multiple of 2.
FP 1: *1 Tss, 1 Tps*, rep from * to *.
RP 1: work all RP in return st.
FP 2: *1 Tps, 1 Tss*, rep from * to *.
Rep FP and RP 1 and 2.

Instructions

The sweater is worked from the top down with one strand of each yarn and finishes with knitted ribbing. Work in rows until the V-neck is closed up, and then in rounds.

YOKE

Using one strand of each yarn and a 7mm (US 10½/11, UK 2) single-ended crochet hook with cable, 51(53:57:59:65:67) ch.

FP 1: starting in the second ch from the hook, pick up sts in back loops of the ch row until you have a total of 51(53:57:59:65:67) sts on the hook.

RP 1: work all RP in return st.

N.B.: work all raglan sts Tps and the sts on either side of the raglan st Tss. Work the increases next to the V-neck immediately before the end st.

Divide the work as follows, placing a marker at each side of every raglan st:

front: 1 end st, 1 st, **raglan:** 1 st, **sleeve:** 11(11:13:13:15:15) sts, **raglan:** 1 st, **back:** 21(23:23:25:27:29) sts, **raglan:** 1 st, **sleeve:** 11(11:13:13:15:15) sts, **raglan:** 1 st, **front:** 1 st, 1 end st.

Begin moss st and raglan increases (see Techniques, pages 148 and 149) in the back loops of FP 2 as follows:

FP 2: front: 1 end st, 1 Tps, inc 1 Tss, **raglan:** 1 Tps, **sleeve:** inc 1 Tss, *1 Tps, 1 Tss, rep from * until 2 sts before marker, 1 Tps, inc 1 Tss, **raglan:** 1 Tps, **back:** inc 1 Tss, *1 Tps, 1 Tss, rep from * until 2 sts before marker, 1 Tps, inc 1 Tss, **raglan:** 1 Tps, **sleeve:** inc 1 Tss, *1 Tps, 1 Tss, rep from * until 2 sts before marker, 1 Tps, inc 1 Tss, **raglan:** 1 Tps, **front:** inc 1 Tss, 1 Tps, 1 end st.

Increase the following number of times on the individual parts including FP 2 round:

Back: inc 1 st at each side of back on foll 31(31:35:34:36:37) FP, then 1(1:–:2:1:1) sts on foll 1(1:–:1:1:1) alt FP (85(87:93:97:101:105) sts).

Each sleeve: inc 1 st each side of sleeve on foll 25(25:27:31:26:29) FP, then on foll 4(4:4:2:6:5) alt FP (69(69:75:79:79:83) sts).

Front:

At both armhole sides: inc 1 st at armhole edges on foll 17(19:21:25:24:25) FP, then on foll 8(7:7:5:7:7) alt FP.

V-neck at both sides: inc 1 st at neck edge on foll 6(8:8:11:11:10) alt FP, then on foll 10(8:9:6:7:9) FP (86(88:94:98:102:106) sts).

When you have worked all the increases for the V-neck, break off the yarn, join the fronts together and work in rounds.

Change to the 7mm (US 10½/11, UK 2) double-ended crochet hook and 2 balls of each yarn.

Place a marker at the start of the round, i.e. in the raglan st at the left side of the back.

Round 1: work the end st at each side of the V-neck at the front tog (dec 1 st).

Continue increasing for the raglan on FP until you have a total of 312(316:340:356:364:380) sts, including the raglan sts.

Divide for the body and sleeves – the raglan sts belong to the front and back.

Work the body first.

BODY

The body consists of 170(174:186:194:202:210) sts plus 1 raglan st at each side of the front and back (174(178:190:198:206:214) sts).

Make 2 ch rows to insert in each armhole on the body (see Techniques, page 166) as follows:

Take two lengths of each yarn, about 15¾in (40cm) long, 11(13:11:11:13:13) ch, break off yarn and pull the end through the last ch (10(12:10:10:12:12) ch).
Place a marker at the centre of the ch sts just made to mark the start of round.
Work 1 round over the sts of the body, picking up sts in the back loops of the ch row in each armhole as follows:

Round 1: pick up 5(6:5:5:6:6) sts in the ch row and work across the front to the second armhole. Pick up 10(12:10:10:12:12) sts in the second ch row and work across the back to the first armhole. Pick up the last 5(6:5:5:6:6) sts (194(202:210:218:230:238) sts).

RP of round 1: dec 1 at each side (192(200:208:216:228:236) sts).
Then continue in rounds in moss st until work measures 21(21½:21:21½: 21½:21¾)in / 53.5(54.5:53.5:54.5: 54.5:55)cm from centre back neck.
Bind (cast) off with sl st, and end the round with 1 sl st in the first st of the round.
Break off the yarn and pull the end through the loop.

SLEEVES
Start at the centre bottom of the armhole in the ch row of the body and place a marker at the start of the round.

Round 1: starting at marker under the arm, pick up 5(6:5:5:6:6) sts from the ch, pick up 2 extra sts where the ch meets the body, pick up 69(69:75:79:79:83) sts left at end of raglan shaping, pick 2 extra sts where the body meets the ch, then pick up 5(6:5:5:6:6) sts from the remaining sts of the ch.

On the RP work the 2 extra sts and the outermost st of the ch at each side together (79(81:85:89:91:95) sts).
Work 1 round.
On the next round dec 1 st on each side of the marker.
Continue in rounds and then dec on each side of marker as follows:
Dec 1 st on foll 4th(4th:3rd:3rd:3rd:3rd) RP 4(5:16:13:13:8) times.
Then dec 1 st on foll 3rd(3rd:2nd:2nd: 2nd:2nd) RP 12(11:2:6:6:13) times (45(47:47:49:51:51) sts).
Continue without shaping until sleeve measures 16⅜(16½:16⅜:15¾: 15¾:15¾)in / 41.5(42:41.5:40:40:40)cm from the armhole.
Bind (cast) off with sl st and finish in the first sl st of the round.
Break off the yarn.
Make the second sleeve in the same way.

FINISHING
Weave in the ends.

BODY RIBBING
Using one strand of each yarn and a 4mm (US 6, UK 8) circular needle, pick up and knit 192(200:208:216:228:236) sts in the bind- (cast-) off round starting at one side of the body.
Place a marker at the start of the round and work 2(2:2½:2½:2½:2½)in / 5(5:6:6: 6:6)cm in k1, p1 rib.
Bind (cast) off with Italian bind- (cast-) off with 2 preparatory rounds (see Techniques, page 170).

SLEEVE CUFFS

Place a marker at the centre underarm of the sleeve at the start of the round.

Using a 4mm (US 6, UK 8) circular knitting needle and one strand of each yarn, pick up and knit 45(47:47:49:51:51) sts in the bound- (cast-) off round.

Round 1: work k1, p1 rib to the last 2 sts of the round, p2tog.

Work a total of 2(2:2¼:2¼:2¼:2¼)in / 5(5:6:6:6:6)cm in k1, p1 rib.

Bind (cast) off with Italian bind- (cast-) off with 2 preparatory rounds.

NECKBAND

Using a 5mm (US 8, UK 6) standard crochet hook and one strand of each yarn, work 1 row sl st along each side of the V-neck immediately before the end sts. Start in the middle of the shoulder at one side of the front and finish at the middle of the shoulder on the opposite side.

Change to a 4mm (US 6, UK 8) circular knitting needle.

Place one marker at the centre back for the start of the round and another in the centre st of the front at the bottom of the V.

N.B.: the centre st of the V must always be a knit st. The number of sts must be divisible by 2. Make sure that you have the same number of sts on each side of the front.

Pick up sts in the back loops of the sl st and **at the same time** inc 1 (inc = yo) after every alt sl st.

On next round work the yarn overs k tbl or p tbl as they fit in the pattern.

Work 1 round k1, p1 rib, in which the last st before and first after the marked st at the bottom of the V are both worked k or p.

On next round, dec on each side of the marked st as follows: rib to last st before the marked st, sl2tog wyib, return the sts to the left needle and work them k3tog tbl.

Rep this dec on every alt round.

Work a total of 6 rounds in k1, p1 rib.

Bind (cast) off with Italian bind- (cast-) off with 2 preparatory rounds.

PRIMULA

Moss stitch sweater with stripes and knitted ribbing

SIZES
US 4(6:8:10:12:14)/UK 8(10:12:14:16:18)

FINISHED MEASUREMENTS
Bust
39¾(42¼:44:46½:48:49¾)in /
101(107.5:111.5:118:122:126.5)cm
Length
24½(24½:24¾:25¼:25¼:25¼)in /
62(62:63:64:64:64)cm

MATERIALS
Yarn
Filcolana Tilia (lace/2-ply) 70% kid mohair,
30% silk, 2(3:3:3:4:5) balls in 348 Rainy
Day (A), 2(2:2:2:3:3) balls in 336 Latte
(B), 2(2:2:2:3:3) balls in 327 Sage (C),
2(2:2:2:3:3) balls in 352 Red Squirrel (D);
1oz/25g/230yd/210m
Tunisian crochet hook (suggested)
5.5mm (US 9, UK 5) double-ended
5.5mm (US 9, UK 5) single-ended
with cable
Circular knitting needle
3mm (US 2/3, UK 11), 24 and 32in (60 and
80cm) cable, (32in/80cm only if you knit
with magic loop)
Double-pointed knitting needles
3mm (US 2/3, UK 11) (if you do not knit
with magic loop)
Stitch markers
Approx. 12

GAUGE (TENSION)
19 sts x 16 rows (FP and RP) = 4 x 4in
(10 x 10cm) in pattern using one strand
Tilia and 5.5mm (US 9, UK 5) Tunisian
crochet hook

SPECIAL TECHNIQUES
Decreasing at both sides on return pass
(see Techniques, page 154)
Raglan increase between 2 stitches
(see Techniques, page 150)
Working in rounds (see Techniques,
page 164)
**Casting on new stitches at the armhole
(when working in rounds)**
(see Techniques, page 166)
**Binding (casting) off/decreasing on
forward pass** (see Techniques, page 143)
Italian bind- (cast-) off (see Techniques,
page 170)

MOSS STITCH
Multiple of 2.
FP 1: *1 Tss, 1 Tps*, rep from * to *.
RP 1: work all RP in return st.
FP 2: *1 Tps, 1 Tss*, rep from * to *.
Rep FP and RP 1 and 2.

STRIPE PATTERN
Work 4½(4½:4¾:4¾:4¾:4¾)in /
11.5(11.5:12:12:12:12)cm in yarns A, B, C
then D, respectively.
Finish the sleeves with yarn B.

Instructions

The sweater is worked from the top down. The borders are knitted last.

YOKE

Using yarn A and a 5.5mm (US 9, UK 5) crochet hook with cable, 100(100:104:104:112:116) ch.

FP 1: start in the second ch from the hook and pick up sts in the back loops of the ch row until you have 100(100:104:104:112:116) sts on the hook. Work back in Tunisian return st.
Place a marker on each side of the raglan sts to divide the work as follows:

half back: 14(14:14:14:15:15) sts, **raglan:** 2 sts, **sleeve:** 17(17:19:19:21:23) sts, **raglan:** 2 sts, **front:** 29(29:29:29:31:31) sts, **raglan:** 2 sts, **sleeve:** 17(17:19:19:21:23) sts, **raglan:** 2 sts, **half back:** 15(15:15:15:16:16) sts.
Work 1 row FP and RP in moss st over all sts, working the raglan sts Tps.

At the same time as working raglan increases and moss st, work short rows, as described in instructions FP 2–5 below, to shape the neck.

N.B.: Applies to all sizes. Work short rows over the first 4 FP and RP while increasing for raglan as follows:

FP 2: start 2 sts before the raglan sts at the left side of the front and finish 2 sts after the raglan sts at the right side of the front. Work 1 Tss, 1 Tps, 1 inc, 2 Tps (raglan sts), 1 inc, *1 Tps, 1 Tss*, rep from * to * until 1 st before raglan sts, 1 Tps, 1 inc, 2 Tps (raglan sts), 1 inc, *1 Tps, 1 Tss*, rep from * to * until 1 st before raglan sts, 1 Tps, 1 inc, 2 Tps (raglan sts), 1 inc, *1 Tps, 1 Tss*, rep from * to * until 1 st before raglan sts, 1 Tps, 1 inc, 2 Tps (raglan sts), 1 inc, 1 Tps, 1 Tss (108(108:112:112:120:124) sts).

FP 3: 2 ch to extend the RP. Starting in the second st before the last crocheted st, work this st and 1 Tps tog (2 ch should lie at the back of the work), *1 Tss, 1 Tps* rep from * to * until raglan sts, 1 inc, 2 Tps (raglan sts), 1 inc, *1 Tps, 1 Tss*, rep from * to * until 1 st before raglan sts, 1 Tps, 1 inc, 2 Tps (raglan sts), 1 inc, *1 Tps, 1 Tss*, rep from * to * until 1 st before raglan sts, 1 Tps, 1 inc, 2 Tps (raglan sts), 1 inc, *1 Tps, 1 Tss*, rep from * to * until 1 st before raglan sts, 1 Tps, 1 inc, 2 Tps (raglan sts), 1 inc, *1 Tps, 1 Tss*, rep from * to * once more and end with 1 Tps.

FP 4: 2 ch to extend the RP. Starting in the second st before the last crocheted st, work this st and 1 Tss tog (2 ch should lie at the back of the work), *1 Tps, 1 Tss* rep from * to * until 1 st before raglan sts, 1 Tps, 1 inc, 2 Tps (raglan sts), 1 inc, *1 Tps, 1 Tss*, rep from * to * until 1 st before raglan sts, 1 Tps, 1 inc, 2 Tps (raglan sts), 1 inc, *1 Tps, 1 Tss*, rep from * to * until 1 st before raglan sts, 1 Tps, 1 inc, 2 Tps (raglan sts), 1 inc, *1 Tps, 1 Tss*, rep from * to * until 1 st before raglan sts, 1 Tps, 1 inc, 2 Tps (raglan sts), 1 inc, *1 Tps, 1 Tss*, rep from * to * three times more, and end with 1 Tps.

FP 5: 3 ch to extend RP. Starting in the third st before the last crocheted st, work this st and 1 Tss tog (3 ch should lie at the back of the work), *1 Tps, 1 Tss* rep from * to * until 1 st before raglan sts, 1 Tps, 1 inc, 2 Tps (raglan sts), 1 inc, *1 Tps, 1 Tss*, rep from * to * until 1 st before raglan sts, 1 Tps, 1 inc, 2 Tps (raglan sts), 1 inc, *1 Tps, 1 Tss*, rep from * to * until 1 st before raglan sts, 1 Tps, 1 inc, 2 Tps (raglan sts), 1 inc, *1 Tps, 1 Tss*, rep from * to * until 1 st before raglan sts, 1 Tps, 1 inc, 2 Tps (raglan sts), 1 inc, *1 Tps, 1 Tss*, rep from * to * five times more, and end with 1 Tps.

Continued on page 40 > >

Work RP in return st, finishing the row with 1 ch. Break off the yarn and pull the end through the ch.

Change to a 5.5mm (US 9, UK 5) double-ended Tunisian crochet hook and 2 balls of yarn.

Work in rounds in stripes in moss st.

Place a marker at the left side of the back between the 2 raglan sts to mark the start of the round.

Inc on each side of the raglan sts from the top of the neck as follows:

Front and back: inc 1 st 26(29:30:34:35:39) times on FP, 1 st 3(2:2:1:1:-) times on alt FP (95(99:101:107:111:117) sts not including raglan sts).

Sleeves: inc 1 st 18(17:16:16:17:19) times on FP, 1 st 7(8:9:10:10:10) times on alt FP (75(75:77:79:83:89) sts not including raglan sts).

At the same time as the raglan increases, change colour as described in stripe pattern below.

When work measures 4½(4½:4¾:4¾:4¾:4¾)in / 11.5(11.5:12:12:12:12)cm from centre back neck, change to yarn B.

Then work stripes of the same width using yarn C, yarn D and yarn A again.

The sleeves end with yarn B.

When all the raglan increases have been worked, 348(356:364:380:396:420) sts (including raglan sts from here on) remain.

Divide the work for body and sleeves.

BODY

Complete the body first.

One of the 2 raglan sts belongs to the body at each side of the front and back. The other belongs to the sleeves.

There are 194(202:206:218:226:238) sts, including 1 raglan st at each side of the front and back.

Make 2 ch rows to insert in each armhole on the body.

Take two lengths of about 15¾in (40cm) of yarn in the same colour as the stripe you are working on.

Make 9(11:13:13:13:11) ch, break off the yarn and pull the end through the last st (8(10:12:12:12:10) ch).

Place a marker at the centre of one ch row to mark the start of the round.

Work 1 round, picking up sts in the back loops of the ch row in each armhole as follows:

Round 1: pick up 4(5:6:6:6:5) sts in the ch row, and continue across the front to the second armhole. Pick up 8(10:12:12:12:10) sts in the second ch row and work across the back to the first armhole. Pick up the last 4(5:6:6:6:5) sts from the ch row (210(222:230:242:250:258) sts).

RP of round 2: dec 1 st at each side (208(220:228:240:248:256) sts).

Then continue without shaping in moss st and stripes until work measures 21¾(21¾:22¼:22¾:22¼:22¼)in / 55(55.5:56.5:57.5:56.5:56.5)cm from centre back neck, or your desired length before ribbing.

Bind (cast) off with sl st, ending the round with 1 sl st in first st. Break off the yarn, and pull the end through the loop.

SLEEVES

Continue in stripes in moss st.

Begin the round at the centre of the ch row in the armhole. Place a marker at the start of the round.

Round 1: pick up 2 extra sts at each side where the ch row meets the body. Place a marker around the 2 extra sts plus the outermost st of the ch row at each side.

On the RP work these sts tog (85(87:91:93:97:101) sts).

Round 2: dec 1 st at centre of underarm (84(86:90:92:96:100) sts).

Continue without shaping in moss st and stripes until sleeve measures 17¼(17¾:18:18:18:17¾)in / 44(45:46:46:46:45)cm from the armhole.

Bind (cast) off with sl st, finishing with 1 sl st in first st.

Break off the yarn and pull the end through the loop.

Make the second sleeve in the same way.

FINISHING
Weave in the ends.

BODY RIBBING
Place a marker at one side for the start
of the round.
With two strands of yarn A and a 3mm (US 2/3,
UK 11) circular knitting needle, pick up and knit
192(204:212:224:232:240) sts from the bound-
(cast-) off round.
Work in rounds in k1, p1 rib, until the border
measures 1½(1½:1½:1½:2:2)in / 4(4:4:4:5:5)cm.
Bind (cast) off with Italian bind- (cast-) off with
2 preparatory rounds.

SLEEVE CUFFS
Place a marker at centre of underarm for the start
of the round.
Using two strands yarn B and a 3mm (US 2/3,
UK 11) 32in (80cm) circular needle (if using magic
loop) or 3mm (US 2/3, UK 11) double-pointed
needles, pick up and knit 76(78:82:84:88:92) sts
from the bound- (cast-) off round.
Round 1: work in k1, p1 rib and dec
28(30:32:34:36:38) sts evenly spaced across the
round (48(48:50:50:52:54) sts).
Work in rounds in k1, p1 rib until border measures
1½(1½:1½:1½:2:2)in / 4(4:4:4:5:5)cm.
Bind (cast) off with Italian bind- (cast-) off with
2 preparatory rounds.

NECKBAND
Place a marker at centre back neck for the start of
the round.
Using two strands yarn A and a 3mm (US 2/3,
UK 11) circular knitting needle, pick up and
knit 100(100:104:104:112:116) sts round the neck
edge on the right side, and **at the same time** inc
24(24:28:28:34:38) sts, evenly spaced, by working
a yo (124(124:132:132:146:154) sts on needle).
Work in rounds in k1, p1 rib until neckband
measures 1in (2.5cm).
Bind (cast) off with Italian bind- (cast-) off with
2 preparatory rounds.
Weave in the last ends.

Summer

MARIGOLD

V-neck glitter top

SIZES
US 4(6:8:10:12:14)/UK 8(10:12:14:16:18)

FINISHED MEASUREMENTS
Bust
39(41¼:43:45¼:46¾:49¼)in /
99(105:109:115:119:125)cm
Hips
41¼(43¾:45¼:47¾:49¼:51½)in /
105(111:115:121:125:131)cm
Length
20¾(21¼:21¼:21¾:22½:22¾)in /
53(54:54:55:57:58)cm

MATERIALS
Yarn
4(4:5:5:6:7) balls of Filcolana Merci
(fingering/4-ply) 50% superwash wool,
50% pima cotton in 610 Gingerbread;
1¾oz/50g/219yd/200m
2(2:2:2:2:2) balls of Kremke Soul Wool
Stellaris (lace/2-ply) 47% viscose, 41%
polyester, 12% metallic yarn in 120 Peach
Silver (shade 120); 1oz/25g/613yd/560m
Tunisian crochet hook (suggested)
5mm (US 8, UK 6) single-ended with cable
or single-ended straight
Standard crochet hook
3.5mm (US 4, UK 9/10)

GAUGE (TENSION)
20 sts x 18 rows (FP and RP) = 4 x 4in
(10 x 10cm) in Tunisian simple st using
one strand of each yarn and 5mm (US 8,
UK 6) Tunisian crochet hook

SPECIAL TECHNIQUES
End stitch at left edge in 1 vertical bar
(see Techniques, page 136)
**Binding (casting) off/decreasing on
forward pass** (see Techniques, page 143)
**Binding (casting) off for armhole with
sl st, both sides** (see Techniques, page 147)
Decreasing at both sides on return pass
(see Techniques, page 154)
Increasing in back vertical bar
(see Techniques, page 152)
Double wheat stitch in a diagonal line
(see Techniques, page 156)
Binding (casting) off with slip stitch in rib
(see Techniques, page 142).

MOSS STITCH
Multiple of 2.
FP 2: *1 Tss, 1 Tps*, rep from * to *.
RP 2: work all RP in return st.
FP 3: *1 Tps, 1 Tss*, rep from * to *.
Rep FP and RP 2 and 3.

CHART

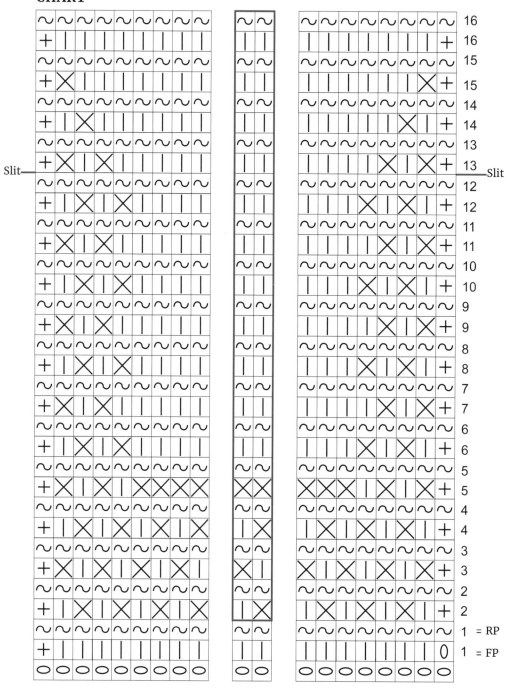

Left side   Centre   Right side

	= Tps
	= Tss
∼	= return st
+	= end st
O	= ch
☐	= pattern repeat (pattern is repeated widthways)

Instructions

Front and back are worked in rows from the bottom up.

BACK

Using one strand of each yarn and 5mm (US 8, UK 6) crochet hook, 105(111:115:121:125:131) ch.

FP 1: start in the second ch from the hook and pick up sts in the back loops of the ch row until you have a total of 105(111:115:121:125:131) sts on the hook.

All RP are worked in return st.

Continue in rows in moss st according to the chart as follows:

FP 2: 1 end st, *1 Tss, 1 Tps, rep from * to the last st before end st, and work 1 Tss, 1 end st.

FP 3: 1 end st, *1 Tps, 1 Tss, rep from * to the last st before end st, and work 1 Tps, 1 end st.

FP 4: as FP 2.

FP 5: 1 end st, 1 Tps, 1 Tss, 1 Tps, 1 Tss, work Tps to the last 4 sts before end st and work 1 Tss, 1 Tps, 1 Tss, 1 Tps, 1 end st.

FP 6: 1 end st, 1 Tss, 1 Tps, 1 Tss, 1 Tps, work Tss to the last 4 sts before end st, and work 1 Tps, 1 Tss, 1 Tps, 1 Tss, 1 end st.

FP 7: 1 end st, 1 Tps, 1 Tss, 1 Tps, work Tss to the last 3 sts before end st and work 1 Tps, 1 Tss, 1 Tps, 1 end st.

Continue following the chart up to and including row 16, but place a marker on row 12 at both sides for the slit.

Continue without shaping in Tss, until work measures 3½(3½:3½:4:4¼:4¼)in / 9(9:9:10:11:11)cm.

Dec 1 st at each side on RP (103(109:113:119:123:129) sts).

Then dec 1 st at each side on foll 15th(15th:15th:15th:16th:16th) RP twice (99(105:109:115:119:125) sts).

Continue without shaping until work measures 11½(11½:11½:11¾:12:12½)in / 29.5(29.5:29.5:30:30.5:31.5)cm.

Bind (cast) off 4(5:5:5:5:6) sts for armhole at each side on next FP as follows:

Work sl st over the first 4(5:5:5:5:6) sts, work to the last 4(5:5:5:5:6) sts, and work sl st over these (91:95:99:105:109:113) sts).

Break off the yarn.

Rejoin yarn to the remaining sts and work back.

Size US 10 (UK 14): work sl st over the first 3 sts, work to last 3 sts and work sl st over these.

All sizes: dec at each side immediately before the end stitch as follows:

Dec -(-:-:-:2:2) sts twice on FP, then dec 1 st on RP 9(10:12:11:11:12) times, and then dec 1 st on alt RP three times (67(69:69:71:73:75) sts).

Continue without shaping, until work measures 19¼(19¾:19¾:20:20½:20¾)in / 49(50:50:51:52:53)cm.

NECK EDGE

Place a marker on either side of the central 17 sts (all sizes) and complete the right side first.

FP 1: work to the first marker and work the 17 sts.

Bind (cast) off 6(6:6:6:6:7) sts at the neck edge on next FP then bind (cast) off 5(5:5:6:6:6) sts on following FP (14(15:15:15:16:16) sts).

Continue without shaping, until work measures 20¾(21¼:21¼:21¾:22½:22¾)in / 53(54:54:55:57:58)cm.

Bind (cast) off with sl st over the remaining sts. Break off the yarn, and pull the end through the last st.

Make the left side in the same way as the right, but reversing all shapings. Break off the yarn, and pull the end through the last st.

FRONT

Work the front as for the back until work measures 12½(12½:12:12½:12½:13)in / 31.5(31.5:30.5:32:31.5:33)cm.

Begin decreasing for the V-neck.

Place a marker in the centre st.

Shoulder on left of the hook

Start the FP in the first st to the left of the centre st and complete the shoulder on the left side of the hook first. Dec at the neck edge on the RP immediately before end st as follows:

Dec 1 st on foll 2(-:-:2:2:-) RP, then on foll 17(19:19:18:18:21) alt RP (14(15:15:15:16:16) sts).

At the same time after the 10th(10th:10th:11th: 11th:12th) dec at the armhole, begin the sloping double wheat st pattern (dwht).

The pattern begins at the armhole side and slopes in towards the neck.

N.B.: the increases for dwht towards the armhole at both sides have changed a little in relation to the example in the photo in order to create a more attractive line over the shoulder.

FP 1: work Tss to the last 3 sts, 1 Tps, 1 wht, 1 end st.

RP 1: work 1 end st, 1 wht, work to end of row in return st.

FP 2: work in Tss to the Tps st before wht, 1 Tps, 1 wht, 1 Tps inc in back loop of end st, 1 end st.

RP 2: work 1 end st, 1 Tps, 1 wht, R2tog, work to end of row in return st.

FP 3: work in Tss to the dec before wht, 1 Tps in both loops that were crocheted tog, 1 wht, 1 Tps, 1 Tks inc in back loop of the Tps, 1 end st.

RP 3: work 1 end st, 1 Tss, 1 Tps, 1 wht, R2tog, work to end of row in return st.

N.B.: from here on, work increases in Tss.

Rep FP and RP 3 until you reach the end st at the neck edge. Then continue in Tss over all sts. Continue decreasing at the neck edge until there are 14(15:15:15:16:16) sts remaining.

Continue without shaping, until work measures 20¾(21¼:21¼:21¾:22½:22¾)in / 53(54:54:55:57:58)cm from the cast-on edge and finish with 1 row sl st.

Break off the yarn and work the other side in the same way, but reversing all shapings.

Shoulder on the right of the hook

Start at the right edge and work until last st before the centre st as follows (this is now your end st):

Dec at the neck edge on the RP immediately before end st as follows:

Dec 1 st on foll 2(-:-:2:2:-) RP, then on foll 17(19:19:18:18:21) alt RP (14(15:15:15:16:16) sts).

At the same time after the 10th(10th:10th:11th:11th:12th) dec at the armhole, begin the sloping double wheat st pattern (dwht). The pattern begins at the armhole side and slopes in towards the neck.

FP 1: work 1 end st, 1 wht, 1 Tps, Tss to end of row.

RP 1: work in return st to dwht, dwht, 1 end st.

FP 2: work 1 end st, 1 inc in ch row between end st and next vertical bar, 1 wht, 1 Tps, Tss to end of row.

RP 2: work in return st to Tss before 1 Tps worked on FP, R2tog, 1 wht, work in return st to end of row.

FP 3: work 1 end st, 1 Tss, inc 1 Tss in back loop of Tps st, 1 Tps, 1 wht, 1 Tps, Tss to end of row.

RP 3: 1 end st, work in return st to wht, 1 wht, R2tog, work in return st to end of row.

N.B.: from here on, work increases in Tss.

Rep FP and RP 3 until you reach the end st at the neck edge. Then continue in Tss over all sts. Continue to work as the first side, but reversing all shapings.

FINISHING

Weave in the ends. Sew up the left shoulder seam first.

Work both armhole bands in rows before sewing up the side seams.

LEFT ARMHOLE BAND

Start at the bottom of the armhole and using a 5mm (US 8, UK 6) Tunisian crochet hook and one strand of each yarn, pick up 99(101:101:103:103:105) sts on the hook around the armhole.

N.B.: if desired, use a 3.5mm (US 4, UK 9/10) crochet hook to help pick up sts on the hook.

Work 1 FP and RP in moss st.

Bind (cast) off with sl st in moss st.

Wait until you have worked the neckband before working the second armhole band.

NECKBAND

Start at the right edge of the shoulder, with the right side of the front facing you and, using a 5mm (US 8, UK 6) Tunisian crochet hook and one strand of each yarn, pick up 119(126:126:128:130:136) sts on the hook as follows: pick up 36(39:39:40:41:42) sts down one side of the neck, 1 st in the bottom of the V, 36(39:39:40:41:42) sts up the other side of the neck and 46(47:47:47:47:51) sts along the back neck.

Work RP in return st, decreasing at the bottom of the V by R3tog (i.e. 1 st on either side of the st at the bottom of the V plus the V st = 1 st). Work 2 FP and RP rows in moss stitch, with the same st of the pattern (Tks or Tps) on each side of the st at the bottom of the V on the FP, and R3tog on the RP at the bottom of the V. Bind off with sl st in moss st.

RIGHT ARMHOLE BAND

Sew up the right shoulder seam and sew the edges of the neckband tog.

Make the second armhole band in the same way as the first.

FINISHING

Sew up both side seams with mattress st from the slit marker up.

With the right side facing you, work 1 row sl st round the edges of the slits at both sides.

Weave in the last ends.

STAR TOP

Short-sleeved top in lace pattern

SIZES
US 2(4:6:8:10:12:14)/UK 6(8:10:12:14:16:18)

FINISHED MEASUREMENTS
Bust
34¼(36¼:38½:41:43:45¼:46½)in /
87(92:98:104:109:115:119)cm
Hips
35¾(37¾:40¼:42½:44½:46¾:48½)in /
91(96:102:108:113:119:123)cm
Length
21¼(21¼:21¼:21¾:21¾:21¾:22)in /
54(54:54:55:55:55:56)cm

MATERIALS
Yarn
4(4:4:5:5:6:6) balls of Filcolana Tilia
(lace/2-ply) 70% kid mohair, 30% silk in
321 Powder Pink; 1oz/25g/230yd/210m
Tunisian crochet hook (suggested)
5mm (US 8, UK 6) single-ended with cable
or single-ended straight
Standard crochet hook
3.5mm (US 4, UK 9/10)
Double-pointed knitting needles
5mm (US 8, UK 6), 24in (60cm) cable
Stitch markers
4

GAUGE (TENSION)
21 sts x 14 rows (FP and RP) = 4 x 4in
(10 x 10cm) in pattern using 5mm (US 8,
UK 6) Tunisian crochet hook

SPECIAL TECHNIQUES
End stitch at left edge in 2 vertical bars
(see Techniques, page 138)
Increasing in back vertical bar
(see Techniques, page 152)
**Binding (casting) off/decreasing on
forward pass** (see Techniques, page 143)
**Binding (casting) off for armhole with
slip stitch, both sides** (see Techniques,
page 147)
Decreasing at both sides on return pass
(see Techniques, page 154)

Instructions

The front, back and sleeves are worked separately in rows from the bottom up.
N.B.: the wrong side of the work is the right side of the garment. This means that when changing yarn the ends must be facing you as you crochet.

BACK

Using a 5mm (US 8, UK 6) Tunisian crochet hook, 95(101:107:113:119:125:129) ch.
N.B.: take care not to crochet too tightly, as the pattern should be able to form a wavy edge at the bottom of the garment.
FP 1: starting in the second ch from the hook, pick up sts in the back loops of the ch row until you have a total of 95(101:107:113:119:125:129) sts on the hook.

RP 1: work in shell rib according to the chart as follows:
Sizes US 2–12 (UK 6–16): work 1 end st, *3 R, 1 ch, R3tog, 1 ch, rep from * to the last 3 sts before end st and work 3 R, 1 end st.
Size US 14 (UK 18): work 1 end st, 2 R, 1 ch, R3tog, 1 ch, *3 R, 1 ch, R3tog, 1 ch, rep from * to the last 2 sts before end st and work 2 R, 1 end st.
FP 2: work in shell rib according to the chart as follows:
Sizes US 2–12 (UK 6–16): work 1 end st, *3 Tps, 1 Tss round ch sp, 1 Tss in top of R3tog, 1 Tss round ch sp, rep from * to last 3 sts before end st and work 3 Tps, 1 end st.

SHELL RIB CHART

Multiple of 6 sts + 3.

N.B.: for size US 14 (UK 18) there are extra stitches before beginning the chart. Refer to written instructions and use chart as a guide for the repeats.

$\boxtimes$ = Tps

$|$ = Tss

$\overline{\lambda}$ = R3tog

$\underline{\iota}$ = Tss round ch sp or in the top of R3tog

$+$ = end st

$\ominus$ = ch

$\square$ = pattern repeat

$\sim$ = return st

Size US 14 (UK 18): work 1 end st, 2 Tps, 1 Tss round the ch sp, 1 Tss in top of R3tog, 1 Tss round ch sp, *3 Tps, 1 Tss round the ch sp, 1 Tss in top of R3tog, 1 Tss round ch sp*, repeat from * to last 2 sts before end st and work 2 Tps, 1 end st.
RP 1 and FP 2 make up pattern.
Continue in pattern without shaping until work measures 1½in (4cm).
In the following section, work the increases and decreases while keeping the pattern correct.
Dec 1 st for hip at each side on next RP (93(99:105:111:117:123:127) sts).
Then dec 1 st at each side on fifth RP once, and 1 st on the foll fourth RP twice (87(93:99:105:111:117:121) sts).

Work 5 FP and RP without shaping.
Inc 1 st at each side on next FP (89(95:101:107:113:119:123) sts).
Then increase 1 st at each side on the following eighth row (91(97:103:109:115:121:125) sts).
Continue without shaping, until work measures 13(12½:12½:12½:12½: 12¼:12½)in / 33(32:32:32:31.5:31.5)cm.
Bind (cast) off 5(5:6:7:6:5:5) sts for the armhole at each side on next FP (81(87:91:95:103:111:115) sts).
Then dec -(-:-:-:-:3:3) sts at each side on next FP, dec -(-:-:-:-:-:2) sts at each side on next two RP, then dec 1 st at each side on following -(2:5:6:11:11:8) RP. Then dec 1 st at each side on next 5(4:2:2:-:-:-) alt RP (71(75:77:79:81:83:85) sts).
Continue without shaping, until work measures 20(20:20:20½:20½:20½:20½)in / 51(51:51:52:52:52:52)cm.
Place a marker on each side of the central 15(17:17:19:19:19:19) sts. Work to the first marker, work sl st over the next 15(17:17:19:19:19:19) sts and work to the end of the FP.
Complete the shoulder at the left end of the hook first. Bind (cast) off 6(7:7:7:7:7:8) sts at the neck edge on next 2(1:1:1:2:2:1) FP, then -(6:6:6:-:-:7) sts on following -(1:1:1:-:-:1) FP (16(16:17:17:17:18:18) sts).
Continue without shaping, until work measures 21¼(21¼:21¼:21¾:21¾: 21¾:22)in / 54(54:54:55:55:55:56)cm.
Bind (cast) off with sl st over the remaining sts. Break off the yarn.
Make the second side in the same way, but reversing all shapings.

FRONT
Make the front as for the back until the work measures 17¼(17¼:17:17¼:17:16½:17)in / 43.5(43.5:43:43.5:43:42:43)cm, and place a marker on each side of the central 15(17:17:19:19:19:19) sts.

Work to the first marker, work sl st over the next 15(17:17:19:19:19:19) sts and complete the FP.

Complete the shoulder on the left end of the hook first.

Bind (cast) off 4(5:5:5:5:5:5) sts at the neck edge on next FP, then 2(2:2:2:2:2:3) sts on next 3(2:2:2:2:2:1) FP, and then -(-:-:-: -:2) sts on next FP.

Then dec 1 st at neck edge on foll 2(4:3:3:4:4:4) RP, and then 1 st on next -(-:1:1:1:1) alt RP (16(16:17:17:17:18:18) sts).

Continue without shaping, until work measures 21¼(21¼:21¼:21¾:21¾: 21¾:22)in / 54(54:54:55:55:55:56)cm.

Bind (cast) off with sl st over the remaining sts. Break off the yarn.

Work the shoulder at the right end of the hook in the same way, but reversing all shapings.

SLEEVES

Using a 5mm (US 8, UK 6) Tunisian crochet hook, make 57(61:65:69:71:75:79) ch.

FP 1: starting in the second ch from the hook, pick up sts in the back loops of the ch row until you have a total of 57(61:65:69:71:75:79) sts on the hook.

RP 1: work in shell rib according to the chart as follows:

Sizes US 2, 8 and 12 (UK 6, 12 and 16): work 1 end st, 2 R, 1 ch, R3tog, 1 ch, *3 R, 1 ch, R3tog, 1 ch, rep from * to last 2 sts before end st, and work 2 R, 1 end st.

Sizes US 4 and 14 (UK 8 and 18): work 1 end st, 4 R, 1 ch, R3tog, 1 ch, *3 R, 1 ch, R3tog, 1 ch, rep from * to last 4 sts before end st and work 4 Tps, 1 end st.

Sizes US 6 and 10 (UK 10 and 14): work 1 end st, *3 R, 1 ch, R3tog, 1 ch, rep from * to last 3 sts before end st, and work 3 R, 1 end st.

FP 2: work in shell rib according to the chart as follows:

Sizes US 2, 8 and 12 (UK 6, 12 and 16): work 1 end st, 2 Tps, 1 Tss round ch sp, 1 Tss in top of R3tog, 1 Tss round ch sp, *3 Tps, 1 Tss round ch sp, 1 Tss in top of R3tog, 1 Tss round ch sp, rep from * to last 2 sts before end st and work 2 Tps, 1 end st.

Sizes US 4 and 14 (UK 8 and 18): work 1 end st, 4 Tps, 1 Tss round ch sp, 1 Tss in top of R3tog, 1 Tss round ch sp, *3 Tps, 1 Tss round ch sp, 1 Tss in top of R3tog, 1 Tss round ch sp, rep from * to last 4 sts before end st and work 4 Tps, 1 end st.

Sizes US 6 and 10 (UK 10 and 14): work 1 end st, *3 Tps, 1 Tss in ch sp, 1 Tss in top of R3tog, 1 Tss in ch sp, rep from * to last 3 sts before end st and work 3 Tps, 1 end st.

RP 1 and FP 2 make up pattern.

Complete RP then work 3 FP and RP in pattern without shaping.

Work the increases and decreases while keeping the pattern correct.

Inc 1 st at each side on the next FP until you have a total of 59(63:67:71:73:77:81) sts.

Complete RP then work 3 FP and RP in pattern without shaping.

Bind (cast) off 5(5:6:6:5:5:5) sts for the armhole at each side on the next FP by working sl st over the first and last 5(5:6:6:5:5:5) sts (49(53:55:59:63:67:71) sts).

Dec at each side as follows:

N.B.: note that you decrease on both FP and RP in the following section, depending on the size.

Dec 1 st at each side on foll 1(2:1:3:5:6:5) RP, then on foll 8(6:8:8:–:4:6) alt RP, then on foll –(1:–:–:1:–:–) third RP, then on foll –(–:–:–:4:–:–) alt RP, then on foll 3(2:5:4:7:8:8) RP, and then dec –(3:–:–:–:–:–) sts on foll –(1:–:–:–:–:–) FP.
There are 25(25:27:29:29:31:33) sts remaining.
Bind (cast) off with sl st over the remaining sts.
Make the second sleeve in the same way.

FINISHING

Remember when making up the garment that the wrong side of the work is the right side of the top.
Weave in the ends.
Using a 3.5mm (US 4, UK 9/10) hook, crochet the shoulder and side seam together with sl st.
Crochet the sleeve seams together and then crochet them to the body with sl st.

I-CORD NECKBAND

Using 5mm (US 8, UK 6) double-pointed needles, cast on 4 sts. *Pick up one st from the sl st row, k3, k2togtbl, slide stitches to the other end of the double-pointed needle, rep from *, bringing the yarn around the back to continue the I-cord. Work I-cord neckband around entire neck opening.
Once you have picked up and worked 100(102:104:106:108:112:116) sts total, bind off the last 4 sts.
Graft the edges of the I-cord together.
Weave in the last ends.

BLEEDING HEART

Tunisian crochet top with glitter stripes and crochet straps

SIZES
US 4(6:8:10:12:14)/UK 8(10:12:14:16:18)

FINISHED MEASUREMENTS
Bust
36¼(38¼:40¼:42¼:44:46)in /
92(97:102:107:112:117)cm
Hips
38(40:42:44:46:48)in /
96.5(101.5:106.5:111.5:116.5:121.5)cm
Length
20¾(21¼:21¼:21¾:22:22½)in /
53(54:54:55:56:57)cm

MATERIALS
Yarn
6(7:7:8:9:10) balls of Permin Elise
(fingering/4-ply) 90% cotton, 10%
cashmere in 881109 Off White (A);
1oz/25g/126yd/115m
1 ball of Lammy Lurex (fingering/4-ply)
100% polyester in 14 Copper (B);
1¾oz/50g/175yd/160m
Tunisian crochet hook (suggested)
6mm (US 10, UK 4) single-ended with cable
or single-end straight
Standard crochet hook
3.5mm (US 4, UK 9/10)

GAUGE (TENSION)
24 sts x 16 rows (FP and RP) = 4 x 4in
(10 x 10cm) in Tunisian cross pattern using
6mm (US 10, UK 4) Tunisian crochet hook

SPECIAL TECHNIQUES
End stitch at left edge in 1 vertical bar
(see Techniques, page 136)
**Binding (casting) off/decreasing on
forward pass** (see Techniques, page 143)
Decreasing at both sides on return pass
(see Techniques, page 154)
Faux I-cord (see Techniques, page 163)

TUNISIAN CROSSED STITCH
Multiple of 2 sts.
(EVEN NUMBER OF STS)
FP 2: *skip 1 st, 1 Tss, 1 Tss in the st you
skipped (1 T-cross st)*, rep from * to *.
RP 2: work in return st.
Rep FP 2 and RP 2.

Instructions

Make the front and back separately in rows from the bottom up.

BACK

Using a 6mm (US 10, UK 4) Tunisian crochet hook and yarn A, 116(122:128:134:140:146) ch.

N.B.: the chain row must not be too loose, as it forms part of the bottom border.

FP 1: start in the second ch from the hook and pick up sts in the back loops of the ch until you have a total of 116(122:128:134:140:146) sts on the hook.

RP 1: work all RP in return st.

Continue in cross pattern as follows:

FP 2: 1 end st, *1 T-cross, rep from * to end, 1 end st.

FP 3 and 4: work as FP 2.

RP 4: change to yarn B and work back along the row.

Break off the yarn.

Change back to yarn A.

Rep FP and RP 2-4 twice more.

You now have 3 stripes in yarn B.

Work the remainder of the top in yarn A.

Continue without shaping in Tunisian crossed st until work measures 3½(3½:3½:3½:3½:4)in / 9(9:9:9:9:10)cm.

Dec 1 st at each side on next RP (114(120:126:132:138:144) sts).

TUNISIAN CROSSED STITCH CHART

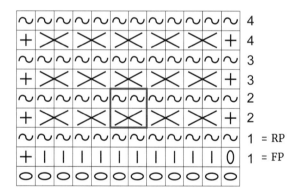

4	
4	
3	
3	
2	
2	
1	= RP
1	= FP

$\boxed{\circ}$ = ch

$\boxed{|}$ = Tss

$\boxed{+}$ = end st

$\boxed{}$ = pattern repeat

$\boxed{\sim}$ = return st

$\boxed{\times}$ = T-cross: skip 1 st, Tss, Tss in skipped st

Then dec 1 st at each side on foll 15th(15th:14th:14th:15th:15th) RP twice (110(116:122:128:134:140) sts).

Continue without shaping until work measures 12½(12½:12¼:12¼:12¼:12½)in / 32(32:31:31:31:32)cm.

Bind (cast) off 6(7:6:6:6:6) sts for the armhole at each side on the next FP as follows:

Work sl st over the first 6(7:6:6:6:6) sts, work to the last 6(7:6:6:6:6) sts and work sl st over these (98(102:110:116:122:128) sts). Break off the yarn.

Join the yarn to the remaining sts and work back.

Then dec at each side immediately before the end st as follows:

N.B.: note that you decrease on both FP and RP in the following section (see Techniques, Binding (casting) off/decreasing on forward pass, page 143, and Decreasing at both sides on return pass, page 154).

Sizes US 4, 6 and 8 (UK 8, 10 and 12): bind (cast) off 2 sts on next FP, dec 1 st on foll 11(11:14:–:–:–) RP, dec 1 st on foll 2(3:2:–:–:–) alt RP.

Size US 10 (UK 14): bind (cast) off 3 sts on next FP, then 2 sts on foll FP, dec 1 st on foll 14 RP, dec 1 st on foll alt RP twice. Work 1 FP and 1 RP.

Size US 12 (UK 16): bind (cast) off 2 sts on next FP twice, dec 1 st on foll 20 RP.

Size US 14 (UK 18): bind (cast) off 3 sts on next FP, then 2 sts on foll three FP, dec 1 st on foll 17 RP. Work 1 FP and 1 RP.

At the same time when work measures 14¾(15:14½:15:15:15)in / 37.5(38:37:38:38:38)cm, bind (cast) off for the neck as follows: place a marker on each side of the central 20(20:22:22:22:22) sts. Work to the first marker, work sl st over the next 20(20:22:22:22:22) sts, work to end of FP (68(70:74:74:74:76) sts).

N.B.: note that you decrease on both FP and RP in the following section.

Complete the shoulder on the left side of the hook first.

Bind (cast) off at the neck edge as follows:

Size US 4 (UK 8): bind (cast) off 3 sts on next four FP, dec 2 sts on foll four RP.

Size US 6 (UK 10): bind (cast) off 4 sts on next FP and dec 3 sts on foll three FP, dec 2 sts on foll four RP.

Sizes US 8, 10 and 12 (UK 12, 14 and 16): bind (cast) off 4 sts on next two FP and dec 3 sts on foll two FP, dec 2 sts on foll four RP.

Size US 14 (UK 18): bind (cast) off 4 sts on next two FP and dec 3 sts on foll three FP, dec 2 sts on foll RP and dec 1 st on foll three RP, dec 1 st on foll alt RP, and work 1 FP and 1 RP.

There are 4 sts remaining.

Work 1 FP, working all 4 sts tog, 1 ch. Break off the yarn, and pull the end of the yarn through the ch.

Complete the shoulder on the right side of the hook in the same way, but reversing all shapings.

FRONT

Work as for the back until work measures 12½(12½:12¼:12¼:12¼:12½)in / 32(32:31:31:31:32)cm.

Bind (cast) off 6(7:6:6:6:6) sts for the armhole at each side on the next FP as for the back (98(102:110:116:122:128) sts).

Then dec at each side immediately before the end st as follows:

N.B.: note that you decrease on both FP and RP in the following section (see Techniques, Binding (casting) off/decreasing on forward pass, page 143, and Decreasing at both sides on return pass, page 154).

Size US 4 (UK 8): bind (cast) off 2 sts on next FP, dec 1 st on foll 11 RP, dec 1 st on foll two alt RP, and work 1 FP and RP.

Sizes US 6 and 8 (UK 10 and 12): bind (cast) off –(2:2:–:–:–) sts on next FP, dec 1 st on foll –(11:14:–:–:–) RP, dec 1 st on foll –(3:2:–:–:–) alt RP, and work 1 FP and RP.

Size US 10 (UK 14): bind (cast) off 3 sts on next FP and dec 2 sts on foll FP, dec 1 st on foll 14 RP, dec 1 st on foll two alt RP, and work 1 FP and RP.

Size US 12 (UK 16): bind (cast) off 2 sts on next two FP, dec 1 st on foll 20 RP, and work 1 FP and RP.

Size US 14 (UK 18): bind (cast) off 3 sts on next FP and 2 sts on foll three FP, dec 1 st on foll 17 RP, and work 1 FP and RP.

At the same time when work measures 14(14¼:14¼:14¼:14¼:14¼)in / 35.5(36:36:36:36:36)cm, bind (cast) off for the neck as follows: place a marker on each side of the central 20(20:22:22:22:22) sts. Work to the first marker, work sl st over the next 20(20:22:22:22:22) sts and work to end of FP.

Complete the shoulder on the left side of the hook first.

Bind (cast) off at the neck edge as follows:

Size US 14 (UK 18) only: bind (cast) off 5 sts on next FP.

All sizes: bind (cast) off –(4:4:4:4:4) sts on foll (–(1:1:1:2:1) FP, and then 3 sts on foll 3(3:3:3:2:1) FP, **at the same time** dec 2 sts on foll 4(3:3:3:3:2) RP, then 1 st on foll 3(2:3:3:1:4) RP, and then 1 st on foll –(–:–:–:1:3) alt RP.

There are 4 sts remaining.

Work 1 FP, working all 4 sts tog, 1 ch. Break off the yarn, and pull the end of the yarn through the ch.

Complete the shoulder at the right side of the hook in the same way, but reversing all shapings.

FINISHING

Weave in all ends.
Using mattress stitch, join the side seams together on the right side.

BOTTOM EDGE

Place a marker at one side for the start of the round.
Using a standard 3.5mm (US 4, UK 9/10) crochet hook, work 1 round sc. Work 1 round sl st on the right side in back loops of the sc all the way round to create a faux I-cord edging. Finish the round with 1 sl st in the first sl st at the start of the round.

EYELET STRAPS

N.B.: there should be an even number of sts around the neck and armhole.

Start at the bottom of the armhole at the right side of the front and work 1 round sl st all the way round the armholes and neck edges with the standard 3.5mm (US 4, UK 9/10) crochet hook. Finish with 1 sl st in the first st at the start of the round.

Place a marker here.

N.B.: when crocheting up sl sts along FP and RP, work 2 sl st for each row.

Work the armhole and strap on the right side of the work as follows:

Round 1: start at the marker at the bottom of the armhole. Work 1 sc in each sl st in both loops up the front to the first point, work 40(42:44:44:46:48) ch to create the shoulder strap. Continue working 1 sc in each sl st from the point on the back down to the marker at the bottom of the armhole.

N.B.: try on the top with the first shoulder strap. If you want the shoulder strap to be a little shorter or longer, this is the time to lengthen or shorten the chain row. Remember that the number of sts must be divisible by 2.

Round 2: 4 ch, *skip 1 st, 1 dc in next st, 1 ch, rep from * to end of round, and finish with 1 sl st in the third ch at the start of the round.

Round 3: 1 ch, *1 sc in the dc, 1 sc round the ch, rep from * to end of round, and finish the round with 1 sl st in the first sc at the start of the round.

Round 4: work 1 sl st in back loop of each st to end of round, to create a faux I-cord edging. Finish with 1 sl st in sl st at the start of the round.

Break off the yarn.

Work around the second armhole in the same way.

EYELET NECKBAND

Place a marker at the left side of the top of the back immediately before the start of the round at the strap.

Round 1: work 1 round sc along the shoulder straps and front and back as follows: *1 sc round the ch, 1 sc in the dc, rep from * to end of round and finish with 1 sl st in the first sc at the start of the round.

Round 2: work 4 ch, *1 dc over dc, 1 ch over ch*, rep from * to * along first shoulder strap, work **1 dc, 1 ch, miss 1 st**, rep from ** to ** across the front, work along the second shoulder strap in the same way as for the first rep from * to *, work across the back in the same way as for the front rep from ** to ** and finish with 1 sl st in the third ch at the start of the round.

Round 3: 1 ch, *1 sc in the dc, 1 sc round ch, rep from * to end of round, and finish the round with 1 sl st in the first sc at the start of the round.

Round 4: work 1 sl st in back loop of each st to end of round, to create a faux I-cord edging. Finish with 1 sl st in sl st at the start of the round.

Break off the yarn.

Weave in the last ends.

DAISY

Top with flowered back

SIZES
One size – US (8–10)/UK (12–14)

FINISHED MEASUREMENTS
Bust
40¼in (102cm)
Hips
42¼in (107cm)
Length
20¾in (53cm)

MATERIALS
Yarn
4 balls of Go Handmade Tencel
Bamboo 'fine' (fingering/4-ply) 40%
tencel, 60% bamboo in 17352 Walnut;
1¾oz/50g/230yd/210m
Tunisian crochet hook (suggested)
5mm (US 8, UK 6) single-ended with cable
or single-ended straight
Standard crochet hooks
3.5mm (US 4, UK 9/10)
3mm (US 2/3, UK 11)
Stitch markers
8

GAUGE (TENSION)
24 sts x 20 rows (FP and RP) = 4 x 4in
(10 x 10cm) in pattern using 5mm (US 8,
UK 6) Tunisian crochet hook

Finished measurements of flower: approx.
3¼ x 3¼in (8 x 8cm) using 3.5mm
(US 4, UK 9/10) standard crochet hook

SPECIAL TECHNIQUES
End stitch at left edge in 1 vertical bar
(see Techniques, page 136)
End stitch at left edge in 2 vertical bars
(see Techniques, page 138)
**Binding (casting) off/decreasing on
forward pass** (see Techniques, page 143)
Decreasing at both sides on return pass
(see Techniques, page 154)

FLOWER
The flower is worked in Tunisian simple st.
Wind the yarn around the tip of your index
finger or a pencil six times.
Fasten the ring of wound yarn in place by
crocheting 1 sl st round it.
Round 1: 1 ch, 18 sc, finish with 1 sl st in
the first sc of the round.
Round 2: 1 ch, 1 sc in first sc, *4 ch, skip
2 sc, work 1 sc, rep from * four more times,
4 ch, skip 2 sc and finish with 1 sl st in the
first sc of the round.
Round 3: flower petals (petal 1):
FP 1: start with 1 sc in the first ch sp, 8 ch.
Starting in the second ch from the hook,
pick up 7 sts on the hook in the back loops
of the ch row until you have a total of 8 sts
on the hook.

Insert the hook under the ch sp, yo and pull the yo through (9 sts on the hook).

N.B.: work the end st on the left side of the flower petal in 2 sts, (see Techniques, End stitch at left edge in 2 vertical bars, page 138).

RP 2: work the sts of the ch sp together with 1 st from the hook (dec 1 st), work the rest of the sts in return st. Work all RP in the same way as RP 1, but there will be 1 st fewer in each row.

Work all FP as for FP 1; you will pick up 1 st fewer in each of the following rows (see chart 1).

When you have worked the last sc of the petal, work 1 sc around the next ch sp (1 sc in next petal).

Make the following five petals in the same way as the first.

When you have worked the last petal, finish the round with 1 sl st in the first sc of the first petal.

CHART 1

Crocheted flower

First petal (1)

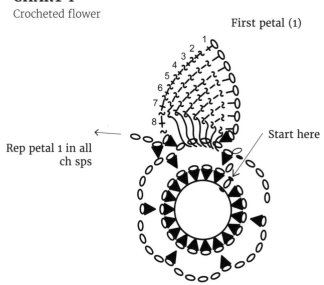

Rep petal 1 in all ch sps

Start here

Crochet		Tunisian Crochet	
= ch		= Tss	
= sl st		= return st	
= sc		= end st	

CHART 2
Crocheted flowered back

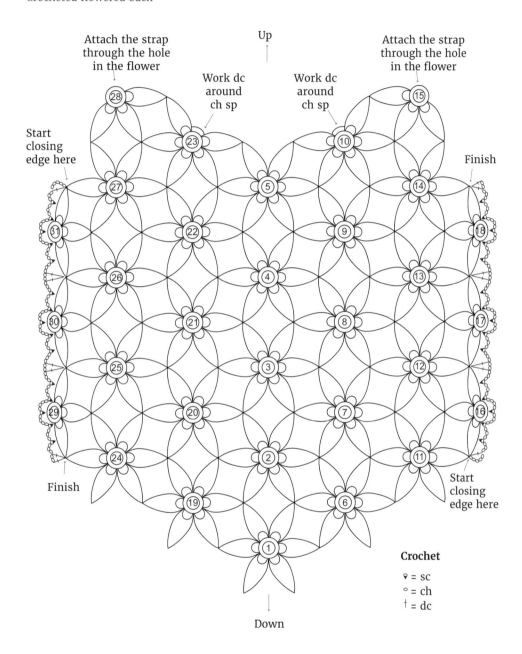

Up

Attach the strap
through the hole
in the flower

Work dc
around
ch sp

Work dc
around
ch sp

Attach the strap
through the hole
in the flower

Start
closing
edge here

Finish

Finish

Start
closing
edge here

Down

Crochet

♀ = sc
° = ch
† = dc

PATTERN
Variation on moss st, multiple of 2.
FP 1: *1 Tss, 1 Tps*, rep from * to *.
RP 1: work all RP in return st.

FP 2: *1 Tss, 1 Tps*.
FP 3: *1 Tps, 1 Tss*.
FP 4: *1 Tps, 1 Tss*.
Rep FP and RP 1–4.

Instructions

The front and sides for the back are worked in one piece.
The flower back is worked separately.

FLOWER BACK

Flower 1: make first flower, see chart 1.
Flower 1 = the flower at the bottom of the point of the back (see chart 2).
Chart 2 shows the entire back and the order in which the flowers are worked.
Join the flowers at the tips with 1 sl st at the end of the 8 ch at the start of the petal, before you complete the first FP and RP.
Flower with 3 petals (flowers 15 and 28 on chart 2): on round 2 (chart 1), where you work ch sps, make 3 ch sps. Then work sl st in both loops of the sc to end of round. Finish with 1 sl st in first sc of first petal. Then make the 3 petals.
Flowers with 5 petals (flowers 10 and 23 on chart 2): in the sixth ch sp work 4 sc around the sp. Finish with 1 sl st in first sc of first petal.
When you have made all the flowers, change to a 3mm (US 2/3, UK 11) crochet hook. Make the closing edge on each side of the back according to chart 2.
Set the work aside until the front is complete.

FRONT AND SIDES

Using a 5mm (US 8, UK 6) Tunisian crochet hook, 157 ch, not too loose.
FP 1: start in the second ch from the hook and pick up sts on the hook in the back loops of the ch row until you have a total of 157 sts.
RP 1: work all RP as return st.
Divide the work into a side piece, a front and a side piece as follows: count 14 sts plus end st into each side and place a marker for the sides.
FP 2: 1 end st, *1 Tss, 1 Tps, rep from * to last st before end st, 1 Tss, 1 end st.
FP 3: 1 end st, *1 Tss, 1 Tps, rep from * to last st before end st, 1 Tss, 1 end st.

FP 4: 1 end st, *1 Tps, Tss, rep from * to last st before end st, 1 Tps, 1 end st.
FP 5: 1 end st, *1 Tps, 1 Tss, rep from * to last st before end st, 1 Tps, 1 end st.
Continue working FP and RP 2–5 without shaping until work is 3½in (9cm) long.
Dec 1 st once on each side of both side markers on next RP (153 sts). Place a new marker between the 2 decreases.
Then dec 1 st on each side of both side markers on the foll eighteenth RP.
Place a new marker between the 2 decreases. There are 145 sts remaining.
Continue without shaping, until work measures 11¼in (28.5cm).
Bind (cast) off at each side as follows:
N.B.: note that you decrease on both FP and RP in the following section.
Bind (cast) off 4 sts once, 3 sts once, 10 sts once, 4 sts once and 3 sts once on foll FP, dec 2 sts seven times on foll alt RP and 2 sts twice on foll RP.
At the same time when work measures 13½in (34.5cm), bind (cast) off for the neck.
Place a marker on each side of the central 23 sts.
Complete the shoulder on the right side of the hook first.
Work in pattern to the first marker and work back. Continue working in rows in pattern over these sts.
Bind (cast) off 3 sts at neck edge three times on foll FP, dec 2 sts once on foll alt RP and 2 sts twice on foll RP (4 sts). Work sl st over the 4 sts.
Complete the left side in the same way, but reversing all shapings.

FINISHING

Weave in the ends.

ARMHOLE EDGES

Work the edges using 3mm (US 2/3, UK 11) standard crochet hook.

Start on the right side of the moss st piece.
Work 1 row sc up to the top of the armhole.
Break off the yarn and pull the end through the last sc.
Work 1 row sl st in both loops of the sc row.
Break off the yarn and pull the end through the last sl st.
Work the second armhole edge in the same way, starting at the top of the armhole and working from right to left.

NECK EDGE

Work 1 row sc. Start at the top of the right side and finish at the top of the left side. Then work 1 row sl st in the same way as for the armhole edges.

CROCHETING THE FRONT AND BACK TOGETHER

Place the front and back wrong sides together and crochet them together on the right side as follows:
using a 3.5mm (US 4, UK 9/10) standard crochet hook, work sc round the ch sp of the back edges edges and the end sts of the front.

SHOULDER STRAPS

Using a 3mm (US 2/3, UK 11) standard crochet hook, join the yarn to the top of the neck and armhole edge and work sc as follows: 1 ch, 4 sc in the 4 sts at the top of the neck and armhole edge, *turn, 1 ch, 4 sc, rep from * until the strap is an appropriate length plus ¾in (2cm) to fold over.
Try the top on as you work to ensure the straps are a suitable length.
Work the second shoulder strap in the same way.
Insert the strap through the hole on the right side of the topmost 3-petal flower on the right side of the back.
Do the same with the left strap.
Adjust the straps, and sew them in place by hand.
Weave in the last ends.

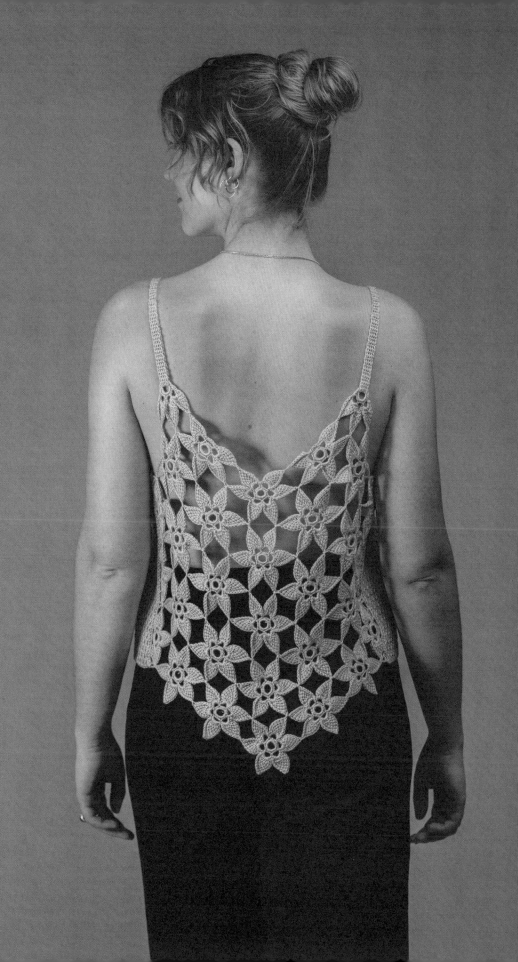

LILY

Short-sleeved, lace pattern top with boat neckline and raglan sleeves

SIZES
US 4(6:8:10:12)/UK 8(10:12:14:16)
FINISHED MEASUREMENTS
Bust
40¼(41¼:44:45¼:48)in /
102(105:112:115:122)cm
Length
19¾(20¾:21¾:21¾:22¾)in /
50(53:55:55:58)cm

MATERIALS
Yarn
4(4:4:4:5) balls of Isager Silk Mohair
(fingering/4-ply), 75% mohair, 25% silk in
shade 0; 1oz/25g/232yd/212m
Tunisian crochet hook (suggested)
5mm (US 8, UK 6) double-ended
5mm (US 8, UK 6) single-ended with cable
or single-ended straight
Standard crochet hook
3mm (US 2/3, UK 11) (for neck border)
Stitch markers
26

GAUGE (TENSION)
20 sts x 14 rows (FP and RP) = 4 x 4in
(10 x 10cm) in pattern using 5mm (US 8,
UK 6) crochet hook

SPECIAL TECHNIQUES
End stitch at left edge in 1 vertical bar
(see Techniques, page 136)
Increasing in back vertical bar
(see Techniques, page 152)
Decreasing at both sides on return pass
(see Techniques, page 154)
**Binding (casting) off/decreasing on
forward pass** (see Techniques, page 143)
Working in rounds (see Techniques,
page 164)

Instructions

The top is worked in rounds from the bottom up to the neck opening. From then on it is worked in rows.

BODY

FP 1 and RP 1 are worked in rows. After that you work in rounds.
Using a 5mm (US 8, UK 6) single-ended crochet hook with cable, 205(210:225:230:245) ch.
N.B.: take care not to make the ch row too tight.

FP 1: start in the second ch from the hook and pick up sts in the back loops of the ch row until you have a total of 205(210:225:230:245) sts on the hook.
RP 1: work in pattern according to the chart as follows: work 1 end st, *1 ch, R3tog, 1 ch, R, rep from * to end.
Continue in rounds. Change to a 5mm (US 8, UK 6) double-ended Tunisian crochet hook and use a second ball of yarn for the RP.
Join the two ends with the right side facing to make a ring and work in rounds in shell rib following the chart without an end st. Place 2 markers at the start of the round.

SHELL RIB VARIATION CHART

Multiple of 5 +3.

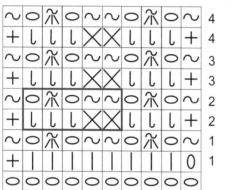

= RP
= FP

X	= Tps	+	= end stitch
I	= Tss	O	= ch
木	= R3tog	□	= pattern repeat
L	= Tss round ch sp or in the top of R3tog	~	= return st

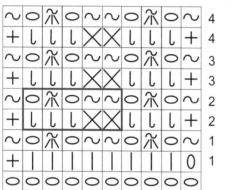

FP 2: *2 Tps, 1 Tss round ch sp, 1 Tss in the top of R3tog, 1 Tss in the ch sp, rep from * to end of round.

Work in rounds as for RP 1 and FP 2 until work measures 10¾(11¾:11¾:11¾:11¾)in / 27(30:30:30:30)cm. Break off the yarn. Set the work aside until you have worked the sleeves.

SLEEVES

Work FP 1 and RP 1 in rows as for the body. Then work in rounds.

Using a single-ended 5mm (US 8, UK 6) Tunisian crochet hook with cable, 58(62:66:70:72) ch.

N.B.: take care not to make the chain row too tight.

FP 1: start in the second ch from the hook, pick up sts in the back loops of the ch row until you have a total of 58(62:66:70:72) sts on the hook.

RP 1: work RP in pattern according to the chart, but without end st.

Continue in rounds. Change to a double-ended 5mm (US 8, UK 6) Tunisian crochet hook and use a second ball of yarn for RP.

The first and last sts of the round are Tps. Place a marker between the 2 Tps (centre underarm).

FP 2: inc 1 in back loop on each side of the 2 Tps (60(64:68:72:74) sts).

Rep these increases on every FP until you have increased a total of 8(8:8:7:8) times and then 1 st twice on alt FP (78(82:86:88:92) sts).

Break off the yarn make the second sleeve in the same way.

YOKE

Divide the body into front and back by placing a marker at each side as follows:

front 102(105:112:115:122) sts, **back** 103(105:113: 115:123) sts.

N.B.: adjust the pattern for the front and back so it is symmetrical either side of the centre front and centre back.

Making the armhole: count 4(5:5:5:5) sts on either side of the marker at each side of the body, and place markers there.

Likewise, count 4(5:5:5:5) sts on either side of the marker at centre underarm and place markers there.

These 8(10:10:10:10) sts on the body and sleeves form the armhole and are missed in the following section.

Place a marker on each side of the raglan sts, which are 1 st from the front, back and sleeves at all four transitions between body and sleeves.

Also place a different-coloured marker between the 2 raglan sts at the left side of the back to mark the start of the round.

The work is now divided into **back:** 93(93:101:103:111) sts, **raglan:** 2 sts, **sleeve:** 68(70:74:76:80) sts, **raglan:** 2 sts, **front:** 92(93:100:103:110) sts, **raglan:** 2 sts, **sleeve:** 68(70:74:76:80) sts, **raglan:** 2 sts.

Work the raglan sts Tps. There are 329(334:357:366:381) sts.

Work in rounds and integrate the decreases into the pattern at each side of the raglan sts.

Dec on each side of the raglan sts as follows:

Back: dec 2 sts on next 1(-:1:1:1) RP and then 1 st on foll 29(30:33:34:36) RP.

Sleeve, back edge: dec 2 sts on 1(2:1:1:1) RP and 1 st on foll 30(29:34:35:37) RP.

Sleeve, front edge: dec 2 sts on foll 1(2:1:1:1) RP, dec 1 st on foll 21(21:23:25:26) on RP and dec 1 st on foll -(-:1:-:2) alt RP.

Front: dec 2 sts on next 1(-:1:1:-) RP and dec 1 st on foll 21(23:25:25:29) RP and dec 1 sts 0(0:1:0:2) alt RP.

At the same time when work measures 15¼(16¼:17¼:18:17¾)in / 38.5(41.5:43.5:46:45)cm, bind (cast) off for the neck.

Break off the yarn and work in rows.

Place a marker at each side of the central 20(19:20:19:20) sts.

Change to a 5mm (US 8, UK 6) single-ended Tunisian crochet hook with cable and start at the left side of the neck.

N.B.: note that you decrease on both FP and RP in the following section.

Bind (cast) off at the neck edge at both sides as follows:

Size US 4 (UK 8): bind (cast) off 9 sts once and 2 sts once on foll FP, dec 1 st twice on foll RP, bind (cast) off 7 st once, 6 sts once and 2 sts once on foll FP, dec 1 st twice on foll alt RP.

Size US 6 (UK 10): bind (cast) off 11 sts once on foll FP, dec 1 st three times on foll RP, bind (cast) off 7 sts once and 6 sts once on foll FP, dec 1 st twice on foll RP and 1 st once on foll alt RP.

Size US 8 (UK 12): bind (cast) off 5 sts twice on foll FP, dec 1 st twice on foll RP and 1 st once on foll alt RP, bind (cast) off 7 sts once and 6 sts once on foll FP, dec 1 st once on foll RP and 1 st twice on foll RP.

Size US 10 (UK 14): bind (cast) off 7 sts once and 5 sts once on foll FP, dec 1 st twice on foll RP and dec 1 st once on foll alt RP, bind (cast) off 5 sts once, 6 sts once and 3 sts once on foll FP, dec 1 st twice on foll alt RP.

Size US 12 (UK 16): bind (cast) off 6 sts once, 5 sts once and 2 sts once on foll FP, dec 1 st once on foll RP, 1 st twice on foll alt RP, bind (cast) off 7 sts once and 5 sts once on foll FP, dec 1 st twice on foll RP, 1 st once on foll alt RP. There are 35(37:35:35:39) sts remaining. Bind (cast) off rem st with sl st. Break off the yarn and pull the end through the last st.

N.B.: you can omit the last row if you want the neckline to be lower at the back.

FINISHING

Weave in the ends. Sew the sleeves and body together at the armhole.

Neckband: using a 3mm (US 2/3, UK 11) crochet hook, work 1 round sc in both loops of the ch row and finish the round with 1 sl st in the first sc at the start of the round. Work a further two rounds sc in the back loops.

Weave in the last ends.

Autumn

IRIS

Skirt with cross stitch embroidery

SIZES
US 4(6:8:10:12:14)/UK 8(10:12:14:16:18)

FINISHED MEASUREMENTS
Waist
31(32¾:35:37¾:40¼:41¾)in /
79(83:89:96:102:106)cm
Hips
39¼(42½:45¼:47¾:50:52)in /
100(108:115:121:127:132)cm
Length
19½(20¾:21¾:22:22:23¼)in /
49.5(53:55:56:56:59)cm

MATERIALS
Yarn
6(6:7:7:8:9) balls of Filcolana Pernilla
(light fingering/3-ply), 100% Peruvian
highland wool in 814 Storm Blue (A);
1¾oz/50g/192yd/175m
1 ball of Krea Deluxe Shiny (fingering/
4-ply) 80% viscose and 20% polyester
in 08 Copper (B); 1oz/25g/104yd/95m
(for embroidery)
Tunisian crochet hook (suggested)
6mm (US 10, UK 4) single-ended with cable
or single-ended straight

Circular knitting needle
4mm (US 6, UK 8), 32in (80cm) cable
Stitch markers
Approx. 20
Elastic
39¼in (1m), max ⅝in (1.5cm) wide
Sewing accessories
Pins and 1 safety pin

GAUGE (TENSION)
19 sts x 16 rows (FP and RP) = 4 x 4in
(10 x 10cm) in pattern using 6mm
(US 10, UK 4) Tunisian crochet hook

SPECIAL TECHNIQUES
End stitch at left edge in 1 vertical bar
(see Techniques, page 136)
Increasing in back vertical bar
(see Techniques, page 152)
Decreasing at both sides on return pass
(see Techniques, page 154)
**Binding (casting) off/decreasing on
forward pass** (see Techniques, page 143)
Binding (casting) off with slip stitch in rib
(see Techniques, page 142)

CHART 1

Moss st for bottom edge and at top by waistband.

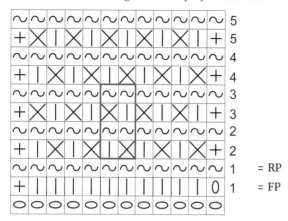

= RP

= FP

☒	= Tps	➕	= end st
		= Tss	◯	= ch
∿	= return st	▢	= pattern repeat

CHART 2

Pattern in Tunisian knit and purl, multiple of 6 + 3.

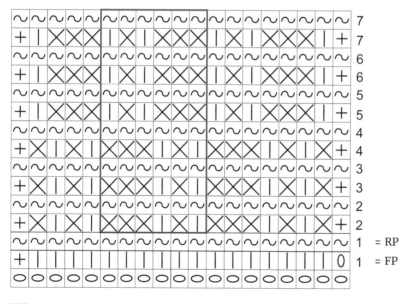

= RP

= FP

☒	= Tps	➕	= end st
		= Tss	▢	= pattern repeat
∿	= return st		

CHART 3

Cross st embroidery. Embroider in the Tps between 2 Tss.

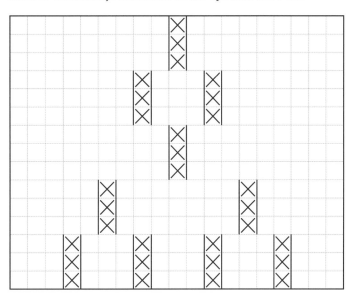

$\boxed{\times}$ = cross stitch in Tps between 2 Tss

Instructions

The front and back are worked in rows from the bottom up.

BACK

Using a 6mm (US 10, UK 4) Tunisian crochet hook, 87(93:99:105:111:117) ch in yarn A, not too loose.

FP 1: start in the second ch from the hook, pick up sts in the back loops of the ch row until you have a total of 87(93:99:105:111:117) sts on the hook.

RP 1: work all RP rows in return st.

FP 2: 1 end st, *1 Tps, 1 Tss, rep from * last st before end st and finish with 1 Tps, 1 end st.

FP 3: 1 end st, *1 Tss, 1 Tps*, rep from * to last st before end st and finish with 1 Tss, 1 end st.

Work a further 2 FP and RP in moss st according to chart 1.

Next FP: work Tps.

From the second FP, continue in pattern according to chart 2 as follows:

FP 2: 1 end st, 1 Tps, *1 Tss, 1 Tps, 1 Tss, 3 Tps, rep from * to last 4 sts before end st and finish with 1 Tss, 1 Tps, 1 Tss, 1 Tps, 1 end st.

RP 2: work all RP in return st.

Work FP and RP 3 and 4 as for FP and RP 2 with Tss over Tss and Tps over Tps.

FP 5: 1 end st, 1 Tss, *3 Tps, 1 Tss, 1 Tps, 1 Tss, rep from * to last 4 sts before end st and finish with 3 Tps, 1 Tss, 1 end st.

Work FP and RP 6 and 7 as for FP and RP 5 with Tss over Tss and Tps over Tps.

Rep FP and RP 2–7 according to chart 2.

At the same time on FP 6, inc 1 st at each side in back loops (89(95:101:107:113:119) sts).

N.B.: work increases and decreases into the pattern.

Then inc 1 st at each side on foll 9th(8th:9th:9th:9th:12th) FP, then 1 st 2(3:3:1:1:2) times on foll 11th(10:10:11:11:14) FP, then -(-:-:1:1:-) st twice on foll 10th FP (95(103:109:115:121:125) sts).

Work in pattern without shaping until the work measures 30(33:34.5:35:35:37)cm / 11¼(13:13½:13¾:13¾:14½)in.

On the next RP dec for the hip at each side as follows:

Dec 1 st at each side of third RP 7(5:6:7:7:8) times, then on next alt RP 3(6:5:4:4:3) times and then on foll RP -(1:1:1:1:1) times (75(79:85:91:97:101) sts).

Next FP: work in Tps.

Work 3 rows without shaping in moss st, see rows 2–4 of chart 1.

Bind (cast) off with sl st in pattern.

The work now measures 19½(20¾:21¾:22:22:23¼)in / 49.5(53:55:56:56:59)cm.

FRONT

Make the front in the same way as the back.

FINISHING

Sew the side seams together with mattress st on the right side.

Weave in the ends.

Inserting the elastic in the waist

Start at one side. On the circular needle, pick up sts in the back loops of the bound-(cast-) off row.

Work 7 rounds in stockinette (stocking) st and bind (cast) off with a stretchy bind-(cast-) off as follows:

k2, return the 2 sts to the left needle, *k2tog, k1, return the 2 sts to the left needle, rep from * to end of round.

Before breaking off the yarn, pull a yarn end twice the length of the waist measurement. Break off the yarn and pull the end through the last st.

Turn the garment wrong side out. Weave the short end in on the wrong side before sewing the casing in place.

Fold the stockinette (stocking) st casing wrong sides together over the skirt. Sew in place on the skirt with whip st, leaving a small opening of about ¾in (2cm). Measure the elastic to the waist plus 1½in (4cm) overlap and pull it though the casing. Sew the elastic together in a ring with 1½in (4cm) overlapping. Sew up the little opening with whip st.

EMBROIDERY

Embroider cross st using yarn B at the bottom right of the front following chart 3.

RHODODENDRON

V-neck sleeveless vest

SIZES
US 4(6:8:10:12:14)/UK 8(10:12:14:16:18)

FINISHED MEASUREMENTS
Bust
39¾(42¼:44½:46½:47¾:50)in /
101(107:113:118:121:127)cm
Hips
42¼(44½:46½:48¾:50:52¼)in /
107(113:118:124:127:133)cm
Length
22(22:22¾:22¾:22¾:23½)in /
56(56:58:58:58:60)cm

MATERIALS
Yarn
4(4:5:5:5:6) balls of Isager Silk Mohair
(fingering/4-ply), 75% mohair, 25% silk in
47 Slate; 1oz/25g/232yd/212m
3(3:4:4:4:4) balls of Isager Alpaca 1
(lace/2-ply) 100% alpaca in Forest;
1¾oz/50g/438yd/400m
Tunisian crochet hook (suggested)
7mm (US 10½/11, UK 2) single-ended with
cable or single-ended straight

Standard crochet hook
3.5mm (US 4, UK 9/10)
Circular knitting needle
3mm (US 2/3, UK 11), 32in (80cm) cable
Stitch markers
Approx. 12

GAUGE (TENSION)
14 sts x 13 rows (FP and RP) = 4 x 4in
(10 x 10cm) in pattern using one strand
of each yarn and 7mm (US 10½/11, UK 2)
Tunisian crochet hook

SPECIAL TECHNIQUES
End stitch at left edge in 1 vertical bar
(see Techniques, page 136)
Increasing in back vertical bar
(see Techniques, page 152)
Decreasing at both sides on return pass
(see Techniques, page 154)
**Binding (casting) off/decreasing on
forward pass** (see Techniques, page 143)
**Binding (casting) off for armhole with
slip stitch, both sides** (see Techniques,
page 147)
Italian bind- (cast-) off (see Techniques,
page 170)
Tunisian rib stitch (T-rib): on FP, Tss,
Tfs (insert hook between Tss just worked
and next st, yarn over, pull through; on RP,
yarn over and pull through 3 loops.

Instructions

The front and back are worked in rows from the bottom up.

BACK

Using one strand of each yarn and 7mm (US 10½/11, UK 2) Tunisian crochet hook, 75(79:83:87:89:93) ch.

FP 1: start in the second ch from the hook and pick up sts in the back loops of the ch row until you have a total of 75(79:83:87:89:93) sts on the hook.

RP 1: work in return st.

FP 2: 1 end st, *1 T-rib, 1 Tps, rep from * to one st before end st, 1 T-rib, 1 end st.

RP 2: work in return st. Remember to pull through 3 loops to close T-rib.
Rep FP and RP 2 throughout the work.

Continue in pattern without shaping until work measures 4¼(4¼:4¾:4¾:4¼:4¼)in / 11(11:12:12:11:11)cm.
Dec 1 st at each side on the next RP (73:77:81:85:87:91) sts).
Then dec 1 st at each side on foll 15th(14th:15th:15th:15th:15th) RP (71(75:79:83:85:89) sts).
Continue without shaping, until work measures 10¼(10¼:10¾:10¼:10¼:10¼)in / 26(26:27.5:26:26:26)cm.

CHART 1

Variation on rib pattern, multiple of 2 + 1.
The pattern looks like knitted fisherman's rib.

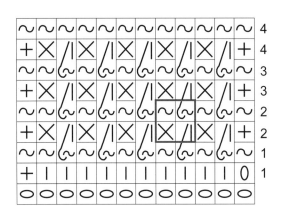

= RP
= FP

⬭ = ch

✕ = Tps

➕ = end st

⌇ = Tss

⟋⟍ = T-rib: on FP, Tss, Tfs (insert hook between Tss just worked and next st, yarn over, pull through; on RP, yarn over and pull through 3 loops)

▢ = pattern repeat

∼ = return st

Work R3tog 3(3:3:4:6:6) times on alt RP and 1(1:1:1:–:–) time on fourth RP (49(51:53:55:55:59) sts).
Continue without shaping, until work measures 19(19:19¾:19¾:19¾:20)in / 48.5(48:50:50:50:51)cm.
Place a marker on either of the central 19(11:13:13:13:13) sts. Work to the first marker, work sl st over the next 19(11:13:13:13:13) sts and work to end of FP.
Complete the left shoulder first. Bind (cast) off 4(8:8:8:8:9) sts at neck edge on next FP (11(12:12:13:13:14) sts).
Continue without shaping, until work measures 20(20:20¾:20¾:20¾:21¼)in / 51(51:53:53:53:54)cm. Work sl st over the remaining sts.
Work the right shoulder as for the left, but reversing all shapings.

FRONT

Work as for the back until work measures 11(10¾:11½:11:11:11)in / 28(27:29:28:28:28)cm.
Continue the armhole shapings in the same way as the back at the same time as the neck shaping.
Armhole shapings as follows:
Work R3tog on foll 3(3:3:4:6:6) alt RP and on 1(1:1:1:–:–) fourth RP (49(51:53:55:55:59) sts).
V-neck
Place a marker in the centre st, and complete shoulder and neck at right side of hook first.
Dec 1 st immediately before end st on alt RP 13(13:14:14:14:15) times (11(12:12:13:13:14) sts).
Continue without shaping until work measures 20(20:20¾:20¾:20¾:21¼)in / 51(51:53:53:53:54) cm.
Work sl st over the remaining sts.
Work the shoulder and neck on the left side of the hook as for the right, but reversing all shapings.

Bind (cast) off 3(4:5:4:3:3) sts for the armhole at each side on the next FP as follows:
work sl st over the first 3(4:5:4:3:3) sts, work to the last 3(4:5:4:3:3) sts and work sl st over these. Break off the yarn. Join the yarn to the remaining 65(67:69:75:79:83) sts and work back in pattern.
Then dec at each side as follows:
place a marker at each side, 6 sts in from the armhole (including end st – the seventh st counted in from the armhole should be Tks).
Then dec at each side after the right side marker and before the left side marker the following number of times:

FINISHING

Sew up the side and shoulder seams
with backstitch.
The bottom, armhole and neck ribbing are
worked in rounds in k1, p1 rib on a 3mm
(US 2/3, UK 11) circular knitting needle with
one strand of each yarn.

BOTTOM RIBBING

Place a marker at one side for the start of
the round.
Using one strand of yarn and a 3mm
(US 2/3, UK 11) circular needle, pick up sts
on the right side of the ch edge as follows:
*pick up 1 st, yo, rep from * all the way
around (298(314:330:346:354:370) sts).
Work in rounds in k1, p1 rib (on round
1 work p tbl in the yo), until the ribbing
measures 2(2:2:2:2:2¼)in / 5(5:5:5:5:6)cm.
Bind (cast) off with Italian bind- (cast-) off
with 2 preparatory rounds.

ARMHOLE RIBBING

Using one strand of each yarn and a
3.5mm (US 4, UK 9/10) crochet hook,
starting at the bottom of the armhole, work
126(130:132:132:136:138) sl st around the
armhole on the right side and join with a
sl st.
Place a marker at the centre bottom of the
armhole for the start of the round. Using
one strand of each yarn and a 3mm (US 2/3,
UK 11) circular knitting needle, work sts in
the front loops of the sl sts as follows:
Round 1 (rib): working in k1, p1 rib, inc
14(14:16:16:18:20) sts evenly spaced, by
wrapping the yarn over the needle and
working k tbl or p tbl in the loop on
the next round until you have a total of
140(144:148:148:154:158) sts.
Work 3 more rounds in rib.
Bind (cast) off with Italian bind- (cast-) off
with 2 preparatory rounds.
Work the second armhole in the same way.

NECK RIBBING

Place a marker at the centre back for the
start of the round, leaving the centre front
marker at the bottom of the V in place.
N.B.: the centre st of the V should always
be a knit st.
The number of sts including the centre st
must be divisible by 2.
Using one strand of each yarn and a 3mm
(US 2/3, UK 11) circular knitting needle,
work sts around the neck edge as follows:
Pick up and knit 31(31:33:33:33:34) sts
across half the back, 52(52:54:54:54:56) sts
down one side of the V-neck, 1 st at
the centre front, 52(52:54:54:54:56) sts
along the other side of the V-neck and
30(30:32:32:32:33) sts across the other half
of the back (166(166:174:174:174:180) sts).
Work 1 round in k1, p1 rib, in which the sts
on each side of the side of the marked st
at the bottom of the V are both either knit
or purl.
On the next round work to the st before the
marked V st and work k3tog tbl over the st
before the marker, the marked V st and the
st after the marker. Rep this dec on every
alt round.
Work a total of 6 rounds in rib
(160(160:168:168:168:174) sts).
Bind (cast) off with Italian bind- (cast-) off
with 2 preparatory rounds.

AFRICAN MARIGOLD

Long-sleeved sweater in lacy pattern

SIZES
US 4(6:8:10:12:14)/UK 8(10:12:14:16:18)

FINISHED MEASUREMENTS
Bust
40¼(42¼:43¾:46½:48:50)in /
102(107:111:118:122:127)cm
Length
23½(23½:23½:24½:24½:24½)in /
60(60:60:62:62:62)cm

MATERIALS
Yarn
5(5:5:6:6:7) balls of Filcolana Tilia
(lace/2-ply), 70% kid mohair and 30% silk
in 352 Red Squirrel; 1oz/25g/230yd/210m
Tunisian crochet hook (suggested)
5mm (US 8, UK 6) double-ended and
5mm (US 8, UK 6) single-ended
with 16in (40cm) cable
Standard crochet hook
3.5mm (US 4, UK 9/10)
Circular knitting needle
4mm (US 6, UK 8), 32in (80cm) cable
Stitch markers
3

GAUGE (TENSION)
18 sts x 10 rows (FP and RP) = 4 x 4in
(10 x 10cm) in pattern using one strand
of yarn and 5mm (US 8, UK 6) Tunisian
crochet hook

SPECIAL TECHNIQUES
End stitch at left edge in 1 vertical bar
(see Techniques, page 136)
Working in rounds (see Techniques,
page 164)
Increasing in back vertical bar
(see Techniques, page 152)
Decreasing at both sides on return pass
(see Techniques, page 154)
**Binding (casting) off for armhole with
slip stitch, both sides** (see Techniques,
page 147)
**Binding (casting) off/decreasing on
forward pass** (see Techniques, page 143)

Instructions

The sweater is worked in rounds from the bottom up to the armholes and then in rows.

The sleeves are worked in rounds from the bottom up to the top shaping, which is worked in rows.

BODY

Work the ribbing first.
Using two strands of yarn and a 4mm (US 6, UK 8) circular knitting needle, cast on 184(192:200:212:220:228) sts. Place a marker at the start of the round.

Work 3 rounds in k1, p1 rib.
Change to a 5mm (US 8, UK 6) double-ended Tunisian crochet hook. Do not break the yarn, but use one ball to work the FP and the second to work the RP.
Work in rounds according to the chart without end sts.
On round 1 (FP 1), pick up the sts onto the Tunisian crochet hook and work RP 1 of the chart (return st).
FP 2: *miss 1 st, Tdc, Tdc in the missed st, rep from * to end of round.
RP 2: work all RP in return st.

CHART

Multiple of 2.

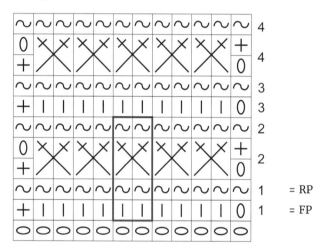

| | = Tss | | | = ch |

| ~ | = return st | | + | = end st |

| ✕✕ | = Tdc-cross: skip 1 st, work the next stitch Tdc and work the skipped stitch Tdc | | ☐ | = pattern repeat |

FP 3: 1 Tss in each st.

Rep FP and RP 2 and 3.

Continue in rounds according to the chart.

Continue without shaping until work measures approx. 13¾(13¾:13½:13¾: 13¾:13¾)in / 35(35:34:35:35:35)cm, ending on RP 3 of the chart.

Divide the work into two groups of 92(96:100:106:110:114) sts for the front and back.

BACK

Change to a 5mm (US 8, UK 6) single-ended Tunisian crochet hook and work in rows.

On the next FP, bind (cast) off 4(4:4:5:5:4) sts for the armhole at each side as follows: work sl st over the first 4(4:4:5:5:4) sts, work to the last 4(4:4:5:5:4) sts of the back and work sl st over these. Break off the yarn. Join the yarn to the remaining 84(88:92:96:100:106) sts and work back. Then dec at each side immediately before the end st as follows:

Size US 4 (UK 8): dec 3 sts each side on foll three alt RP and then dec 2 sts each side on next alt RP.

Sizes US 6 and 8 (UK 10 and 12): dec 3 sts each side on foll four alt RP.

Size US 10 (UK 14): dec 2 sts each side on foll two RP and then dec 3 sts on foll three alt RP.

Size US 12 (UK 16): dec 3 sts on each side on foll five alt RP.

Size US 14 (UK 18): dec 2 sts each side on foll eight RP.

There are 62(64:68:70:70:74) sts remaining. Continue without shaping until work measures 22¾(22¾:22¾:23½: 23½:23½)in / 58(58:58:60:60:60)cm at centre back ending with RP 2.

Place a marker at each side of the central 24(24:24:26:28:28) sts. Work to the first marker, work sl st over the next 24(24:24:26:28:28) sts and work to end of FP.

Complete the shoulder and neck on the left side of the hook first.

On the next FP, bind (cast) off 5 sts at the neck edge (14(15:17:17:16:18) sts).

Continue without shaping until work measures 23½(23½:23½:24½: 24½:24½)in / 60(60:60:62:62:62)cm.

Bind (cast) off with sl st over the remaining sts.

Complete the shoulder and neck at the right side of the hook in the same way as the left, but reversing all shapings.

FRONT

Work as for the back until work measures 18½(18½:17¾:18½:18:18)in / 47(47:45:47:46:46)cm. Bind (cast) off for the neck as follows:

place a marker at each side of the central 14(14:14:14:16:16) sts.

Work to the first marker, work sl st over the next 14(14:14:14:16:16) sts and work to the end of the FP.

N.B.: note that you bind (cast) off on FP and RP respectively.

Complete the shoulder and neck on the left side of the hook first. Bind (cast) off for the neck as follows.

Sizes US 4 and 6 (UK 8 and 10): bind (cast) off 7 sts on next FP and dec 1 st on foll RP, and then dec 1 st on foll two alt RP.

Size US 8 (UK 12): bind (cast) off 7 sts on next FP and dec 1 st on foll three alt RP.

Size US 10 (UK 14): bind (cast) off 5 sts on next FP, then 3 sts on foll FP, and then dec 1 st on foll three RP.

Size US 12 (UK 16): bind (cast) off 7 sts on next FP, and dec 1 st on foll two RP and then 1 st on foll two alt RP.

Size US 14 (UK 18): bind (cast) off 4 sts on next FP, then 3 sts on foll FP, and then dec 2 sts on foll two alt RP.

There are 14(15:17:17:16:18) sts remaining.

Change to a 5mm (US 8, UK 6) double-ended Tunisian crochet hook. Do not break the yarn. Use one ball to work the FP and the second ball to work the RP.

Work in rounds as for the body.

On round 1 (FP 1), pick up the sts onto the crochet hook, increasing 1 st each side of the marker, and then work back according to RP 1 of the chart.

Continue working in rounds according to the chart.

At the same time, inc 1 st once at each side of the marker.

Then inc as follows:

Sizes US 4 and 6 (UK 8 and 10): inc 1 st on foll 7(6:-:-:-:-) third FP, then 1 st on foll 3(4:-:-:-:-) fourth FP, and then 1 st on foll alt FP.

Size US 8 (UK 12): inc 1 st on foll 12 third FP, and then 1 st on foll alt FP.

Size US 10 (UK 14): inc 1 st on foll 2 alt FP, then 1 st on foll 11 third FP, and then 1 st on foll FP.

Sizes US 12 and 14 (UK 16 and 18) inc 1 st on foll -(-:-:-:3:9) alt FP, 1 st on foll -(-:-:-:10:6) third FP and then 1 st on foll alt FP. There are 70(72:76:78:80:84) sts on the hook.

Continue without shaping, until work measures 16¼(16¼:16½:16½:16½:16½)in / 41(41:42:42:42:42)cm.

Change to a 5mm (US 8, UK 6) single-pointed hook with cable and work in rows.

On next FP bind (cast) off for top of sleeve at each side as follows:

work sl st over the first 4(5:5:4:4:4) sts, work to the last 4(5:5:4:4:4) sts and work sl st over these. Break off the yarn.

Join the yarn to the remaining 62(62:66:70:72:76) sts and work back.

Dec for top of sleeve at each side, immediately before the end st as follows:

N.B.: note that you decrease on both FP and RP in the following section.

Continue without shaping, until work measures 23½(23½:23½:24½: 24½:24½)in / 60(60:60:62:62:62)cm. Work sl st over the remaining sts. Complete the shoulder and neck at the right side of the hook in the same way, but reversing all shapings.

SLEEVES

Work the ribbing first.

Using two strands of yarn and a 4mm (US 6, UK 8) circular knitting needle, cast on 46(48:48:48:50:50) sts. Place a marker at the start of the round.

Work 3 rounds in k1, p1 rib.

Size US 4 (UK 8): dec 2 sts on foll three RP, then 1 st on foll alt RP, then 1 st on foll seven RP and then 2 sts on foll three RP.

Size US 6 (UK 10): dec 2 sts on foll two alt RP, then 2 sts on foll RP, then 1 st on foll six RP, then 2 sts on foll two alt RP and then 4 sts on foll FP.

Size US 8 (UK 12): dec 2 sts on foll three RP, then 1 st on foll alt RP, then 1 st on foll seven RP, then 3 sts on foll alt RP and then 4 sts on next FP.

Size US 10 (UK 14): dec 2 sts on foll three RP, then 2 sts on foll RP, then 1 st on foll seven RP, then 2 sts on foll alt RP, then 2 sts on foll RP and then 4 sts on foll FP.

Size US 12 (UK 16) dec 2 sts on foll three RP, then 1 st on foll seven RP, then 1 st on foll two alt RP and then 2 sts on foll four RP.

Size US 14 (UK 18): dec 2 sts on foll four alt RP, then 1 st on foll seven RP, then 1 st on foll third RP, then 2 sts on foll two RP and then 4 sts on foll FP.

There are 22(22:24:24:26:28) sts remaining. Bind (cast) off with sl st over the remaining 22(22:24:24:26:28) sts. Break off the yarn. Make the second sleeve in the same way.

FINISHING

Use a 3.5mm (US 4, UK 9/10) crochet hook, place the pieces right sides together and crochet the shoulders together with sl st. Crochet the sleeves in place in the armholes with sl st in the same way.

NECKBAND

Place a marker at each side of the centre 24(24:24:26:28:28) sts of the back, and at each side of the centre 14(14:14:14:16:18) sts of the front. Place a marker in the centre of the back sts to mark the start of round.

Starting at the start-of-round marker and using two strands of yarn and a 4mm (US 6, UK 8) circular knitting needle, pick up 12(12:12:13:14:14) sts across the back, 42(43:43:43:43:46) sts on the side of the neck, 14(14:14:14:16:18) sts across the neck, 42(43:43:43:43:46) sts on the side of the neck, and finally the last 12(12:12:13:14:14) sts across the back.

There are 122(124:124:126:130:136) sts. Work 6 rounds in k1, p1 rib. Bind (cast) off on next round. Break off the yarn. Weave in the ends.

GRAPE HYACINTH

Ribbed sweater with diagonal lines and beads

SIZES
US 4(6:8:10:12:14)/UK 8(10:12:14:16:18)

FINISHED MEASUREMENTS
Bust
39(40½:42½:44:46¾:48½)in /
99(103:108:112:119:123)cm
Hips
40½(42½:44:46¾:48½:50½)in /
103(108:112:119:123:128)cm
Length
22¾(22¾:23½:23½:23½:24½)in /
58(58:60:60:60:62)cm

MATERIALS
Yarn
7(7:8:8-9:9:10) balls of Filcolana
Pernilla (light fingering/3-ply), 100%
Peruvian highland wool in 812 Granite;
1¾oz/50g/192yd/175m
Tunisian crochet hook (suggested)
6mm (US 10, UK 4) single-ended with cable
or single-ended straight
Standard crochet hook
3.5mm (US 4, UK 9/10)
Circular knitting needle
3mm (US 2/3, UK 11), 24in (60cm) cable
Stitch markers
8
Beads
96 silver, size 3-5mm

GAUGE (TENSION)
18 sts x 15 rows (FP and RP) = 4 x 4in
(10 x 10cm) in pattern using 6mm (US 10,
UK 4) Tunisian crochet hook

SPECIAL TECHNIQUES
End stitch at left edge in 1 vertical bar
(see Techniques, page 136)
Increasing in back vertical bar
(see Techniques, page 152)
Decreasing at both sides on return pass
(see Techniques, page 154)
**Binding (casting) off/decreasing on
forward pass** (see Techniques, page 143)
Faux I-cord (see Techniques, page 163)
Italian bind- (cast-) off (see Techniques,
page 170)

RIB PATTERN
Multiple of 2 + 1.
FP 1: work Tss.
RP 1: work all RP in return st.
FP 2: *1 Tps, 1 Tss*, rep from * to *.
Rep RP 1 and FP 2.

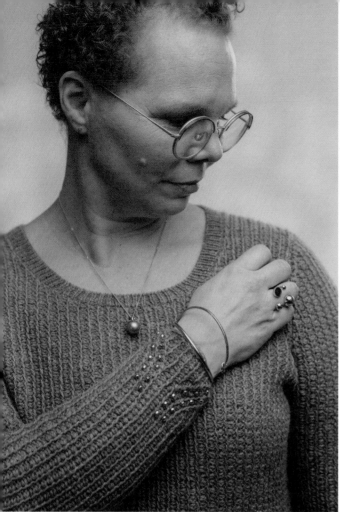

Instructions

The front, back and sleeves are worked separately in rows. The neckband is knitted in rib.

BACK

Using a 6mm (US 10, UK 4) Tunisian crochet hook, 93(97:101:107:111:115) ch.

FP 1: start in the second ch from the hook and pick up sts in the back loops of the ch row until you have a total of 93(97:101:107:111:115) sts on the hook.

RP 1: work in return st.

Continue in rib pattern.

At the same time, divide the work for the diagonal lines as follows:

Count 7(9:11:11:13:15) sts into each side, excluding end st, and place a marker, count a further 5 sts in at each side, and place another marker.

The 5 sts will form the diagonal lines as you dec on the RP towards the centre, and inc on the FP towards each side.

The 5 sts forming the diagonal line at each side are worked 1 Tss, 1 Tps, 1 Tss, 1 Tps, 1 Tss, on every FP on both sides of the garment until the required length.

FP 2: 1 end st, work in rib pattern, until 1 st before the first marker, inc 1 st according to the pattern in back loop, 1 Tps in front loop, work the 5 sts as described above, continue in rib pattern until the third marker, work the 5 sts as described, inc 1 Tps in back loop, 1 st according to pattern in front loop, continue in rib pattern to end of row.

RP 2: R to the 5 marked sts, R 4 sts, R2tog, R to 1 st before the next 5 marked sts, R2tog, and continue working R to end of row.

Rep FP 2 and RP 2, adapting the inc sts into the pattern.

Inc and dec 1 st on every FP and RP on either side of the 5 marked sts at both sides ten times. Then inc and dec 1 st on every second FP and RP six times. Adapt the rib pattern to the decreases and increases. **At the same time,** dec 1 st at each side on foll 24th(24th:24th:16th:24th:25th) RP 2(2:2:3:2:2) times (89(93:97:101: 107:111) sts).

Then continue without shaping or diagonal lines in rib pattern until work measures 13½(13½:14¼:14¼:13¾:14¼)in / 34.5(34.5:36:36:35:36)cm.

On next FP bind (cast) off 5(5:5:5:6:5) sts for the armhole at each side as follows: work sl st over the first 5(5:5:5:6:5) sts, work to the last 5(5:5:5:6:5) sts and work sl st over these. Break off the yarn. Join the yarn to the remaining 79(83:87:91: 95:101) sts and work back in pattern.

Then dec at each side immediately before end st as follows:

dec 1(1:1:1:1:2) sts at each side on foll 3(5:7:9:10:1) RP and then 1 st on foll 4(3:2:1:1:11) alt RP (65(67:69:71:73:75) sts). Continue without shaping until work measures 21½(21½:22¼:22¼:22¼:23)in / 54.5(54.5:56.5:56.5:56.5:58.5)cm from the centre back neck.

Place a marker at each side of the central 15(15:15:17:17:17) sts. Work to the first marker, work sl st over the next 15(15:15:17:17:17) sts and work to end of FP. Complete the shoulder on the left side of the hook first. Bind (cast) off at the neck edge 5(6:6:6:6:6) sts on the foll 2(1:1:1:1:2) FP and then -(5:5:5:5:-) sts on next -(1:1:1:1:-) FP (15(15:16:16:17:17) sts). Continue without shaping, until work measures 22¾(22¾:23½:23½: 23½:24½)in / 58(58:60:60:60:62)cm. Bind (cast) off with sl st. Break off the yarn.

Work the shoulder at the right side of the hook in the same way, but reversing all shapings.

FRONT

Work as for the back until work measures 18(17¾:18:18:17¾:18½)in / 45.5(45:46:46:45:47)cm.

Place a marker at each side of the central 15(15:15:17:17:17) sts. Work to the first marker, work sl st over the next 15(15:15:17:17:17) sts and work to end of FP. Complete the shoulder on the left side of the hook first.

N.B.: note that you decrease on both FP and RP in the following section.

Bind (cast) off at the neck edge as follows:

Sizes US 4 and 10 (UK 8 and 14): bind (cast) off 4 sts on next FP, then 3 sts on foll FP, and then dec 1 st on foll 3(-:-:4:-:-) alt RP.

Sizes US 6 and 8 (UK 10 and 12): bind (cast) off 4 sts on next FP, then 3 sts on foll FP, and then dec 1 st on foll -(1:2:-:-:-) RP, and then 1 st on foll -(3:2:-:-:-) alt RP.

Size US 12 (UK 16): bind (cast) off 2 sts on foll 3 FP, then dec 1 st on foll 2 RP, then 1 st on foll 2 alt RP, and then 1 st foll third RP.

Size US 14 (UK 18): bind (cast) off 4 sts on next FP, then 2 sts on foll 2 FP, then dec 1 st on foll three alt RP, and then 1 st on foll third RP.

There are 15(15:16:16:17:17) sts remaining. Work sl st over the remaining sts.

Make the shoulder at the right side of the hook in the same way, but reversing all shapings.

SLEEVES

Using 6mm (US 10, UK 4) Tunisian crochet hook, 39(41:41:43:43:45) ch.

FP 1: start in the second ch from the hook and pick up sts in the back loops of the ch row until you have a total of 39(41:41:43:43:45) sts on the hook.

RP 1: work in return st.

Continue in rib pattern. Divide the work for diagonal lines as follows:

count 5(7:7:9:9:11) sts in at each side, excluding end st, and place a marker, count a further 5 sts in at each side and place a marker.

The 5 sts will form the diagonal lines as you dec on the RP towards the centre, and inc on the FP towards each side.

The 5 sts forming the diagonal line at each side are worked 1 Tss, 1 Tps, 1 Tss, 1 Tps, 1 Tss, all the way up on the FP.

FP 2: 1 end st, work in rib pattern until 1 st before the first marker, inc 1 st according to the pattern in back loop, 1 Tps in front loop, work the 5 sts as described above, continue in rib pattern until the third marker, work the 5 sts as described, inc 1 Tps in back loop, 1 st according to the pattern in front loop, continue in rib pattern to end of row.

RP 2: R to the 5 marked sts, R 4, R2tog, work to 1 st before next 5 marked sts, R2tog, R to end of row.

Inc and dec 1 st on every FP and RP respectively at each side of the 5 marked sts at both sides ten times. Then inc and dec 1 st on foll six alt FP and RP.

At the same time, inc at each side immediately before the end st as follows: inc 1 st on foll 5th(5th:4th:4th:4th:3rd) FP 10(9:7:15:15:5) times, then 1 st on foll 3rd(4th:5th:–:2nd:4th) FP 2(3:5:– :1:12) times, and then 1 st –(–:2:–:– :–) times on foll –(–:4th:–:–:–) FP (63(65:69:73:75:79) sts).

Continue without shaping, until work measures 17(17¼:17¼:17¼:17¼:17¼)in / 43(44:44:44:44:44)cm.

On next FP, bind (cast) off 5(5:5:5:6:5) sts for top of sleeve at each side as follows: Work sl st over the first 5(5:5:5:6:5) sts, work to the last 5(5:5:5:6:5) sts, and work sl st over these. Break off the yarn. Join the yarn to the remaining 53(55:59:63: 63:69) sts and work back.

Then dec at each side, immediately before the end st as follows:

Size US 4 (UK 8): dec 1 st each side on next RP, then on foll eight alt RP and then on foll six RP six.

Size US 6 (UK 10): dec 1 st each side on foll three RP, then 1 st on next alt RP, then 1 st on foll third RP, then 1 st on foll fourth RP four times, then on next third RP, then 1 st four times on foll fourth RP and then dec 2 sts on next RP.

Size US 8 (UK 12): dec 1 st on each side on foll five RP, then 1 st on foll six alt RP and then 1 st on foll six RP.

Size US 10 (UK 14): dec 1 st on each side on foll four RP, then on foll seven alt RP, then on foll six RP, and then 2 sts on next RP.

Size US 12 (UK 16): dec 1 st on each side on foll three RP, then on foll seven alt RP and then eight RP.

Size US 14 (UK 18): dec 1 st on each side on foll five RP, then on foll seven alt RP, then on next fourth RP, then on foll four RP and then 3 sts on next RP.

There are 23(23:25:25:27:29) sts remaining. Bind (cast) off with sl st in pattern over the remaining sts. Break off the yarn.

Make the second sleeve in the same way.

FINISHING

Weave in the ends.

Sew on beads with ordinary sewing thread along the diagonal lines on the front and sleeves.

On the front, sew 2 x 12 beads on each side and on the sleeves sew 2 x 6 beads on each side on every alt row.

Join the sleeve and side seams with mattress st with the right sides out.

Using a 3.5mm (US 4, UK 9/10) crochet hook, crochet the shoulder seams together with sl st. Join the sleeve seams in the same way.

BOTTOM EDGE OF BODY AND SLEEVES

Using a 3.5mm (US 4, UK 9/10) crochet hook, make a faux I-cord by working 1 round sl st in back loops of the ch row at the bottom edge of the body and sleeves.

N.B.: take care not to work the sl st too tightly.

NECKBAND

Using a 3mm (US 2/3, UK 11) circular knitting needle and with right side facing, pick up and knit sts around neck.

N.B.: pick up and knit 2 sts in the end st of each row down each side of the neck at the front. Pick up and knit 1 st in each st along the bound (cast) off edges at the front and back neck working an inc by working a yo after every third st. Work the yo k tbl or p tbl on the next round as fits the pattern. Place a marker at the start of the round. Work 6 rounds in k1, p1 rib. Bind (cast) off with Italian bind- (cast-) off with 2 preparatory rounds.

Weave in the last ends.

Winter

WINTER JASMINE

Textured V-neck sweater

SIZES
US 4(6:8:10:12:14)/UK 8(10:12:14:16:18)

FINISHED MEASUREMENTS
Bust
39(41:43:45:46¾:48¾)in /
99(104:109:114:119:124)cm
Hips
41¾(43¾:45¾:47¾:49½:51½)in /
106(111:116:121:126:131)cm
Length
23½(23½:23½:23½:24½:24½)in /
60(60:60:60:62:62)cm

MATERIALS
Yarn
4(4:5:5:6:6) balls of Isager Highland Wool
(light fingering/3-ply) 100% wool in Sand;
1¾oz/50g/301yd/275m (A)
5(6:6:7:7:8) balls of Isager Silk Mohair
(lace/2-ply) 75% kid mohair, 25% silk in
Shade 6; 1oz/25g/232yd/212m (B)
1 ball of Kremke Stellaris (lace/2-ply) 47%
viscose, 41% polyester, 12% metallic yarn
in 180 Beige Silver; 1oz/25g/613yd/560m for
the neckband (C)
Tunisian crochet hook (suggested)
7mm (US 10½/11, UK 2) single-ended
straight or single-ended with cable

Standard crochet hook
4mm (US 6, UK 8)
Double-pointed knitting needles
5mm (US 8, UK 6)
Stitch markers
3 or more

GAUGE (TENSION)
16 sts x 13 rows (FP and RP) = 4 x 4in
(10 x 10cm) in pattern using one strand
of each yarn and 7mm (US 10½/11, UK 2)
Tunisian crochet hook

SPECIAL TECHNIQUES
End stitch at left edge in 2 vertical bars
(see Techniques, page 138)
Increasing in back vertical bar
(see Techniques, page 152)
Decreasing at both sides on return pass
(see Techniques, page 154)
**Binding (casting) off/decreasing on
forward pass** (see Techniques, page 143)
Faux I-cord (see Techniques, page 163)

PATTERN
Tunisian crossed stitch with purl
FP 2: *3 T-cross (1 T-cross = skip 1 st,
1 Tss, 1 Tss in the skipped st), Tps 3*, rep
from * to *.
RP 2: work all RP in return st.
Rep FP 2 and RP 2.

Instructions

The front and back are worked in rows with one strand of each yarn.

BACK

Using one strand of yarn A and one strand of yarn B, and a 7mm (US 10½/11, UK 2) Tunisian crochet hook, 85(89:93:97:101:105) ch.

FP 1: start in the second ch from the hook and pick up sts in the back loops of the ch row until you have a total of 85(89:93:97:101:105) sts on the hook.

RP 1: work all RP in return st.

On next FP work the pattern as follows, so that the 3 Tps sts of the pattern fall on the centre 3 sts of the back.

FP 2: 1 end st, 7(9:2:4:6:8) Tps, *3 T-cross, 3 Tps, rep from * to last 7(9:2:4:6:8) sts before end st and work 7(9:2:4:6:8) Tps, 1 end st.

Continue without shaping until work measures 3½(3½:3½:3¼:3¼:3¼)in / 9(9:9:8:8:8)cm.

Dec 1 st for the hip at each side on next RP (83(87:91:95:99:103) sts).

Then dec 1 st at each side on foll 3rd(3rd:3rd:3rd:4th:4th) RP 3(3:3:3:1:1) times then on foll 2nd(2nd:2nd:2nd:3rd:3rd) RP twice, and then on foll -(-:-:-:2nd:2nd) RP -(-:-:-:2:2) times (73(77:81:85:89:93) sts).

CHART

Multiple of 9 + 6.

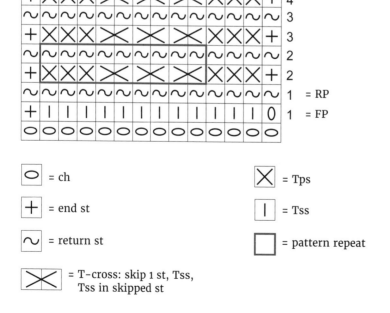

⬯ = ch	✕ = Tps
+ = end st	│ = Tss
∿ = return st	▢ = pattern repeat
✕ = T-cross: skip 1 st, Tss, Tss in skipped st	

There are 57(59:61:63:65:67) sts remaining.
Continue without shaping until work measures 22¾(22¾:22¾:22¾:23:23)in / 58(58:58:58:58.5:58.5)cm from the centre back neck.
Place a marker at each side of the centre 13(13:13:13:13:15) sts. Work to the first marker, work sl st over the next 13(13:13:13:13:15) sts, work to end of FP. Complete the shoulder on the left side of the hook first.
Bind (cast) off 8(9:9:10:10:9) sts for the neck on next FP (14(14:15:15:16:17) sts). Continue without shaping, until work measures 23½(23½:23½:23½: 24½:24½)in / 60(60:60:60:62:62)cm.
Bind (cast) off with sl st over the remaining 14(14:15:15:16:17) sts.
Work the shoulder on the right side of the hook in the same way, but reversing all shapings.

FRONT

Make the front in the same way as the back until work measures 15¼(14½:14¼:13¾:14½:14½)in / 38.5(37:36:35:37:37)cm.
Continue the armhole shapings in the same way as the back at the same time as the neck shaping.
Place a marker in the centre st and complete each side separately by decreasing for the V-neck.
Place a marker in the eighth st from the centre st.
Work the 8 sts at the neck edge as follows to make a patterned neckline: 1 end st, 6 T-cross, 1 Tps. Decreasing in the ninth st from the neck edge all the way up creates a patterned border up the side of the V-neck. Complete the shoulder and neck at the right side of the hook first.
Dec 1 st at the neck edge on foll 2(2:1:2:1:1) RP and then on foll 12(13:14:14:15:15) alt RP (14(14:15:15:16:17) sts).
Bind (cast) off by working 1 row sl st over the remaining 14(14:15:15:16:17) sts.

Work 3 FP and RP without shaping.
On next FP inc 1 st at each side (75(79:83:87:91:95) sts).
Then inc 1 st at each side on foll 7th(7th:7th:6th:7th:7th) FP twice (79(83:87:91:95:99) sts).
Continue without shaping, until work measures 14½(14½:14½:13¾:14½:13¾)in / 37(37:37:35:37:35)cm.
On next FP, bind (cast) off 4(5:5:4:4:4) sts for the armhole at each side as follows: work sl st over the first 4(5:5:4:4:4) sts, work to the last 4(5:5:4:4:4) sts and work sl st over these. Break off the yarn. Join the yarn to the remaining 71(73:77:83:87:91) sts and work back in return st.
Then dec 1 st at each side immediately before the end st on foll 5(4:7:9:10:12) RP and then on foll 2(3:1:1:1:–) alt RP.

Make the shoulder and neck at the left side of the needle in the same way, but reversing all shapings.

SLEEVES

Using one strand of yarn A and one strand of yarn B, and a 7mm (US 10½/11, UK 2) Tunisian crochet hook, make 34(36:36:36:38:38) ch.

FP 1: start in the second ch from the hook and pick up sts in back loops of the ch row until you have a total of 34(36:36:36:38:38) sts on the hook.

RP 1: work all RP in return st.

On the next FP work the pattern so that the 3 T-cross sts align with the 6 centre sts (applies to all sizes), as follows:

FP 2:

Size US 4 (UK 8): 1 end st, 4 Tps, *3 T-cross, 3 Tps, rep from * to the last 10 sts before end st and work 3 T-cross, 4 Tps, 1 end st.

Sizes US 6, 8 and 10 (UK 10, 12 and 14): 1 end st, 1 T-cross, 3 Tps, *3 T-cross, 3 Tps, rep from * to the last 5 sts before end st, and work 3 Tps, 1 T-cross, 1 end st.

Sizes US 12 and 14 (UK 16 and 18): 1 end st, 1 Tps, 1 T-cross, 3 Tps, *3 T-cross, 3 Tps, rep from * to the last 3 sts before end st, 1 T-cross, 1 Tps, 1 end st.

Continue in pattern without shaping and work a further 4(4:3:2:2:2) FP and RP.

On the next FP, inc 1 st immediately before the end st at both sides (36(38:38:38:40:40) sts). Then inc 1 st at each side on foll 5th(5th:4th:3rd:3rd:3rd) FP 9(9:4:1:1:4) times, then on foll -(-:5th:4th:4th:4th) FP -(-:6:12:12:9) times, and then on foll 2nd(4th:4th:-:-:2nd) FP 1(1:1:-:-:1) time (56(58:60:64:66:68) sts).

Continue without shaping, until work measures 17(17:17¼:17:17:17)in / 43(43:44:43:43:43)cm.

On the next FP, bind (cast) off 4 sts for the armhole at each side as follows:
work sl st over the first 4 sts, work to the last 4 sts and work sl st over these. Break off the yarn. Join the yarn to the remaining 48(50:52:56:58:60) sts and work back in pattern.

Dec at each side before end st as follows:

Sizes US 4, 6 and 8 (UK 8, 10 and 12): dec 1 st at each side on foll three RP, then six times on

foll alt RP, then on next RP, then on next alt RP and then on foll four RP.

Size US 10 (UK 14): dec 2 sts at each side on foll three alt RP, then dec 1 st on foll five alt FP, then dec 2 sts on foll two alt RP and then dec 2 sts on next RP.

Size US 12 (UK 16): dec 2 sts on foll three alt RP, then dec 1 st on foll four alt RP, then dec 1 st on foll two RP, then dec 1 st on next alt RP and then dec 1 st on foll four RP.

Size US 14 (UK 18): dec 2 sts on foll three alt RP, then dec 1st on foll four alt RP, then dec 1 st on foll two RP and then dec 2 sts on foll three alt RP.

There are 18(20:22:22:24:24) sts remaining.

Bind (cast) off with sl st over the remaining sts.

Make the second sleeve in the same way.

FINISHING

Weave in the ends.

Place the pieces right side together and crochet the shoulder, side and sleeve seams together with sl st.

Crochet the sleeves in place in the armholes in the same way.

NECKBAND

Start from the centre back so the join isn't visible from the front, making sure you pick up the same number of sts at each side of the dec in both the front and back loops of every end st.

Using one strand of each yarn and 5mm (US 8, US 6) double-pointed needles, cast on 4 sts.

Pick up one st from the neck edge, slide sts to the right end of the double-pointed needle, bring the yarn around the back and k3, k2togtbl, rep from * to * until centre stitch of the V-neck. Pick up one st from centre of V-neck and one st from next st, slide sts to the right of the needle, k3, k3togtbl (this way the V remains sharp). Rep from * to * around rest of neck opening. Work I-cord neckband around entire neck opening. Once you have worked all the way around, bind (cast) off the last 4 sts.

Break off the yarn and graft the edges of the I-cord together.

Weave in the ends.

ROSEMARY

Long jacket with wheat stitch pattern and raglan sleeves

SIZES
US 4(6:8:10:12:14)/UK 8(10:12:14:16:18)

FINISHED MEASUREMENTS
Bust
42¼(43¾:46¼:47¾:50¼:51½)in /
107.5(111:117.5:121:127.5:131) cm
Length
37½(37½:39¼:39¼:39¼:39¼)in /
95(95:100:100:100:100)cm

MATERIALS
Yarn
10(10:11:11:12:13) balls of Filcolana Tilia
(lace/2-ply), 70% kid mohair, 30% silk in
319 Blue Violet; 1oz/25g/230yd/210m
10(10:11:11:12:13) balls Filcolana Arwetta
Classic (fingering/4-ply), 80% superwash
merino wool, 20% nylon in 143 Denim Blue;
1¾oz/50g/230yd/210m
Tunisian crochet hook (suggested)
9mm (US 13, UK 00) single-ended
with cable
Standard crochet hooks
7mm (US 10½/11, UK 2)
8mm (US 11, UK 0)
Stitch markers
12

GAUGE (TENSION)
12 sts x 9 rows (FP and RP) = 4 x 4in
(10 x 10cm) in pattern using one strand of
each yarn and 9mm (US 13, UK 00)
Tunisian crochet hook

SPECIAL TECHNIQUES
End stitch at left edge in 2 vertical bars
(see Techniques, page 138)
End stitch at left edge in 1 vertical bar
(see Techniques, page 136)
Increasing in back vertical bar
(see Techniques, page 152)
**Casting on new stitches at the
armhole (when working in rounds)**
(see Techniques, page 166)
Decreasing at both sides on return pass
(see Techniques, page 154)
Double wheat stitch in rib (see Techniques,
page 160)

DOUBLE WHEAT STITCH RIB
Multiple of 4 + 3 sts.
FP 1: work Tss.
RP 1: work in return st.
FP 2: *3 Tps, 1 wht*, rep from * to *.
RP 2: work in return st, working the 6 sts
of the wht together (applies to all RP).
FP 3: *3 Tps, 1 wht round the previous
wht*, rep from * to *.
Rep FP and RP 2 and 3.

Instructions

The jacket is worked in rows from the top down with one strand of each yarn.

The body is worked in one piece.

YOKE

Using one strand of each yarn and a 9mm (US 13, UK 00) crochet hook, 59(65:65:67:71:75) ch.

FP 1: starting in the second ch from the hook, pick up sts in the back loops of the ch row until you have a total of 59(65:65:67:71:75) sts on the hook.

RP 1: work back in return st.

Divide the work into **front:** 10(11:11:11:13:13) sts, **raglan:** 3 sts, **sleeve:** 5(7:7:7:7:7) sts, **raglan:** 3 sts, **back:** 17(17:17:19:19:23) sts, **raglan:** 3 sts, **sleeve:** 5(7:7:7:7:7) sts, **raglan:** 3 sts, **front:** 10(11:11:11:13:13) sts (59(65:65:67:71:75) sts).

Always work the raglan sts: 1 Tps, 1 wht, 1 Tps.

FP 2: work in pattern as follows:

Size US 4 (UK 8):
Front: 1 end st, 2 Tps, 1 wht, 3 Tps, 1 wht, 2 Tps; **raglan:** 1 Tps, 1 wht, 1 Tps; **sleeve:** 2 Tps, 1 wht, 2 Tps; **raglan:** 1 Tps, 1 wht, 1 Tps; **back**: 2 Tps, *1 wht, 3 Tps*, rep from * to * twice more, 1 wht, 2 Tps; **raglan:** 1 Tps, 1 wht, 1 Tps; **sleeve:** 2 Tps, 1 wht, 2 Tps; **raglan:** 1 Tps, 1 wht, 1 Tps; **front:** 2 Tps, 1 wht, 3 Tps, 1 wht, 2 Tps, 1 end st.

Sizes US 6 and 8 (UK 10 and 12):
Front: 1 end st, 3 Tps, 1 wht, 3 Tps, 1 wht, 2 Tps; **raglan:** 1 Tps, 1 wht, 1 Tps; **sleeve:** 3 Tps, 1 wht, 3 Tps; **raglan:** 1 Tps, 1 wht, 1 Tps; **back:** 2 Tps, *1 wht, 3 Tps*, rep from * to * twice more, 1 wht, 2 Tps; **raglan:** 1 Tps, 1 wht, 1 Tps; **sleeve:** 3 Tps, 1 wht, 3 Tps; **raglan:** 1 Tps, 1 wht, 1 Tps; **front:** 2 Tps, 1 wht, 3 Tps, 1 wht, 3 Tps, 1 end st.

Size US 10 (UK 14):
Front: 1 end st, 3 Tps, 1 wht, 3 Tps, 1 wht, 2 Tps; **raglan:** 1 Tps, 1 wht, 1 Tps; **sleeve:** 3 Tps, 1 wht, 3 Tps; **raglan:** 1 Tps, 1 wht, 1 Tps; **back:** 1 Tps, *1 wht, 3 Tps*, rep from * to * three times more, 1 wht, 1 Tps; **raglan:** 1 Tps, 1 wht, 1 Tps; **sleeve:** 3 Tps, 1 wht, 3 Tps; **raglan:** 1 Tps, 1 wht, 1 Tps; **front:** 2 Tps, 1 wht, 3 Tps, 1 wht, 3 Tps, 1 end st.

Size US 12 (UK 16):
Front: 1 end st, 1 Tps, 1 wht, 3 Tps, 1 wht, 3 Tps, 1 wht, 2 Tps; **raglan:** 1 Tps, 1 wht, 1 Tps; **sleeve:** 3 Tps, 1 wht, 3 Tps; **raglan:** 1 Tps, 1 wht, 1 Tps; **back:** 3 Tps, *1 wht, 3 Tps*, rep from * to * three times more; **raglan:** 1 Tps, 1 wht, 1 Tps; **sleeve:** 3 Tps, 1 wht, 3 Tps; **raglan:** 1 Tps, 1 wht, 1 Tps; **front:** 2 Tps, 1 wht, 3 Tps, 1 wht, 3 Tps, 1 wht, 1 Tps, 1 end st.

Size US 14 (UK 18):
Front: 1 end st, 1 Tps, 1 wht, 3 Tps, 1 wht, 3 Tps, 1 wht, 2 Tps; **raglan:** 1 Tps, 1 wht, 1 Tps; **sleeve:** 3 Tps, 1 wht, 3 Tps; **raglan:** 1 Tps, 1 wht, 1 Tps; **back:** 3 Tps, *1 wht, 3 Tps*, rep from * to * four times more; **raglan:** 1 Tps, 1 wht, 1 Tps; **sleeve:** 3 Tps, 1 wht, 3 Tps; **raglan:** 1 Tps, 1 wht, 1 Tps; **front:** 2 Tps, 1 wht, 3 Tps, 1 wht, 3 Tps, 1 wht, 1 Tps, 1 end st.

RP 2: work back in pattern.

Inc at each side of the raglan sts, working the increases into the pattern:

Back: inc 1 st each side of back on foll 16(17:20:19:23:20) times FP and then on foll 3(3:2:3:1:3) alt FP (55(57:61:63:67:69) sts).

Sleeves: inc 1 st on foll 18(17:18:19:21:22) FP and then on foll 2(3:3:3:2:2) alt FP (45(47:49:51:53:55) sts).

Front: inc 1 st on foll 12(11:14:15:15:16) FP and then on foll 5(6:5:5:5:5) alt FP (27(28:30:31:33:34) sts).

Work 1 FP and 1 RP.

There are 12 raglan sts in total (3 sts per raglan x 4). Total sts including raglan sts = 211(219:231:239:251:259) sts.

Divide for the body and sleeves.

BODY

The back and front are worked in one piece. Add 2 of the 3 raglan sts at each side to the back (59(61:65:67:71:73) sts) and front (29(30:32:33:35:36) sts). The remaining 1 st of the raglan sts at each side belong to the sleeves (47(49:51:53:55:57) sts).

There are 117(121:129:133:141:145) sts in total for the body.

Make 2 ch rows to insert in the armholes of the body. Take two lengths of about 16in (40cm) of each yarn for each armhole ch. Using a 9mm (US 13, UK 00) crochet hook, work 7 ch. Break off the yarn and pull the end through the seventh ch (6 ch).

FP 1: work across the first front plus 2 raglan sts, pick up sts in back loops of the ch row, miss last raglan st, the sleeve sts and first raglan st, work across 2 raglan sts, the back plus the last 2 raglan sts to the second armhole, pick up sts in the back loops of the second ch row, miss last raglan st, the sleeve sts and first raglan st, and work across 2 raglan sts and the second front.

There are 129(133:141:145:153:157) sts in total for the body.

Continue in rows in pattern without shaping, until work measures 35¾(35¾:37¾:37¾:37¾:37¾)in / 91(91:96:96:96:96)cm from the centre back neck.

Bind (cast) off with sl st. Break off the yarn.

SLEEVES

The sleeves are worked in rows. Place a marker at the centre of the bottom edge of each sleeve. This marker will be used for measuring the length.

Work the end st at the left side of the sleeves in 1 vertical bar.

Make a ch row to insert at the left side of the sleeve.

Take a length of each yarn of about 16in (40cm). Using a 9mm (US 13, UK 00) crochet hook, work 4 ch. Break off the yarn and pull the end through the fourth ch (3 ch).

Inc 3 sts at each side as follows: join yarn to right side of sleeve and work 3 ch, starting in second ch from the hook, pick up 1 st in back loops of the next 2 ch, continue in pattern across the sleeve, insert the ch row at the left side and pick up 3 sts on the hook in the back loops of the ch (53(55:57:59:61:63) sts).

Work back in return st.

Work a further 1 FP and RP before dec begin.

Dec 1 st once at each side immediately before end st.

Then dec 1 st at each side on foll 5(5:3:-: -:-) fourth RP, then on foll 4(4:7:11:9:9) third RP, and then on foll 1(1:1:1:4:4) alt RP (31(33:33:33:33:35) sts).

The sleeve measures 16¼(16¼:16½:16½: 16½:16½)in / 41(41:42:42:42:42)cm from the marker. Bind (cast) off with sl st over the remaining sts. Break off the yarn.

Make the second sleeve in the same way.

FINISHING

Sew up the sleeve seams with mattress st and sew them into the armholes. Weave in the ends.

SLEEVE EDGES

Using one strand of each yarn and a 7mm (US 10½/11, UK 2) standard crochet hook, work 1 round sc on the right side in the sl st.

EDGE ALL ROUND THE NECK, CENTRE FRONT AND BOTTOM EDGES

Start at the centre back.
Using one strand of each yarn and 7mm (US 10½/11, UK 2) standard crochet hook, work 1 round sc on the right side.
At each corner at the top and bottom of the fronts work 3 sc in the same st to make sharp corners.

FRONT AND NECK EDGES

Change to an 8mm (US 11, UK 0) standard crochet hook.
Divide a ball of each yarn into four equally-sized balls (eight balls in total).
N.B. – Important!: place the yarns next to one another in pairs (one strand of each). Start at the bottom edge of the right front. With all eight strands and the right side facing you, work 1 row sl st in between the sc and the jacket itself. Work up along the front and around the neck to the centre back. Break off the yarn. Pull the strands through to the wrong side.
Work in the same way from the bottom of the left front, up the front edge and around the neck to the centre back. Break off the yarn and pull the ends through the last sl st.
Sew around the last sl st of the opposite sl st row, so it looks like a sl st and pull the ends through to the wrong side.
Weave in the ends.

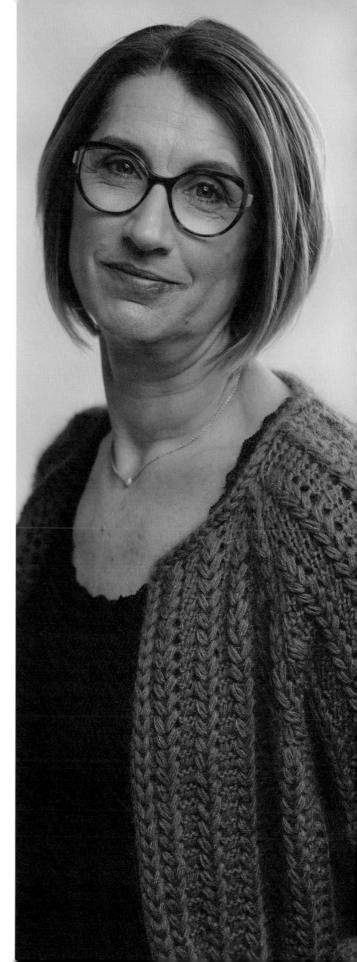

DAHLIA

Roll-neck sweater with raglan sleeves

SIZES
US 4(6:8:10:12:14)/UK 8(10:12:14:16:18)

FINISHED MEASUREMENTS
Bust
40¼(42¼:44:46:48:50)in /
102(107:112:117:122:127)cm
Length
24¼(24½:24¾:25¼:25½:25½)in /
61.5(62.5:63:64:64.5:65)cm

MATERIALS
Yarn
6(7:7:7:8:9) balls of Filcolana Anina (fingering/
4-ply) 100% superwash merino wool in
357 Sumac; 1¾oz/50g/230yd/210m
6(7:7:7:8:9) balls of Filcolana Tilia
(lace/2-ply) 70% kid mohair, 30% silk
in 350 Sienna; 1oz/25g/230yd/210m
Tunisian crochet hook (suggested)
7mm (US 10½/11, UK 2) double-ended
7mm (US 10½/11, UK 2) single-ended with cable
Standard crochet hook
5mm (US 8, UK 6)
Stitch markers
12

GAUGE (TENSION)
16 sts x 13.5 rows (FP and RP) = 4 x 4in
(10 x 10cm) in pattern using one strand of each
yarn and 7mm (US 10½/11, UK 2) Tunisian
crochet hook

SPECIAL TECHNIQUES
End stitch at left edge in 1 vertical bar
(see Techniques, page 136)
Raglan increase between 2 stitches
(see Techniques, page 150)
**Casting on new stitches at the armhole (when
working in rounds)** (see Techniques, page 166)
Decreasing at both sides on return pass
(see Techniques, page 154)
Working in rounds (see Techniques, page 164)
Binding (casting) off with slip stitch in rib
(see Techniques, page 142)

PATTERN 1
Tunisian rib:
FP 1: *2 Tss, 2 Tps*, rep from * to * to end
of round.
RP 1: work all RP in return st.
Rep FP 1 and RP 1.

PATTERN 2
Variation on moss st:
FP 1: *1 Tss, 1 Tps*, rep from * to *.
RP 1: work all RP in return st.
FP 2 and 3: work Tss over Tss and Tps over Tps.
FP 4: *1 Tss, 1 Tps*, rep from * to *.
FP 5 and 6: work Tps over Tps and Tss over Tss.
Rep FP and RP 1–6.

Instructions

The sweater is worked in rounds from the top down with one strand of each yarn and a double-ended Tunisian crochet hook.

The roll collar, the bottom border of the sweater and the sleeve borders are worked in rib.

ROLL COLLAR

Using one strand of each yarn and a 5mm (US 8, UK 6) standard crochet hook, 76(80:84:84:84:88) ch.

N.B.: take care not to make the chain too tight.

Change to a 7mm (US 10½/11, UK 2) double-ended Tunisian crochet hook. Join the ch row into a ring and work in rounds, using another ball of each yarn for the RP.

Round 1: work 1 round in Tss.

Place a marker at the start of the round.

Round 2: work rib according to pattern 1.

Work in rounds in rib until work measures 4¾in (12cm).

Turn the roll collar wrong side out (this is now the right side of the sweater) and work around the opposite way.

Work Tss over Tss and Tps over Tps. Continue without shaping until the roll collar measures 7in (18cm).

Work 1 round Tps. Break off the yarns.

YOKE

Inc for the raglan between 2 vertical bars and work the raglan sts Tps in the yoke. Divide the work and place a marker at each side of the raglan sts = 8 markers.

Back: 23(23:25:25:25:27) sts; **raglan:** 2 sts; **sleeve:** 11(13:13:13:13:13) sts; **raglan:** 2 sts; **Front:** 23(23:25:25:25:27) sts; **raglan:** 2 sts; **sleeve:** 11(13:13:13:13:13) sts; **raglan:** 2 sts.

Change to a 7mm (US 10½/11, UK 2) Tunisian crochet hook with cable and work in rows according to pattern 2, with short rows as described below, while **at the same time** increasing for the raglan.

N.B.: applies to all sizes. Work short rows over FP and RP 1–3, turning with 1/2/2 sts at each side of the neck on the front.

FP 1:

Front: start in the first st before raglan sts at the left side of the **front:** 1 Tps, 1 inc, 2 Tps (raglan sts), 1 inc; **sleeve:** 1 Tps, *1 Tss, 1 Tps*, rep from * to * to next raglan, 1 inc, 2 Tps (raglan sts), 1 inc; **back:** 1 Tps, *1 Tss, 1 Tps*, rep from * to * to next raglan, 1 inc, 2 Tps (raglan sts), 1 inc; **sleeve:** 1 Tps, *1 Tss, 1 Tps*, rep from * to * to next raglan, 1 inc, 2 Tps (raglan sts), 1 inc; **front:** 1 Tps, work 2 ch (84(88:92:92:92:96) sts).

RP 1: work all RP in return st.

FP 2:

Front: 2 ch to extend the RP. Starting in the second st before the last crocheted st, work this st and 1 Tps tog (2 ch should lie at the back of the work), 1 Tss, 1 Tps, 1 inc, 2 Tps (raglan sts), 1 inc; **sleeve:** *1 Tss, 1 Tps* rep from * to * to next raglan, 1 inc, 2 Tps (raglan sts), 1 inc; **back:** 1 Tps, *1 Tss, 1 Tps*, rep from * to * to next raglan, 1 inc, 2 Tps (raglan sts), 1 inc; **sleeve:** 1 Tps, *1 Tss, 1 Tps*, rep from * to * to next raglan, 1 inc, 2 Tps (raglan sts), 1 inc; **front:** 1 Tps, 1 Tss, 1 Tps.

FP 3:

Front: 2 ch to extend the RP. Starting in the second st before the last crocheted st, work this st and 1 Tps tog (2 ch should lie at the back of the work), 1 Tss, 1 Tps, 1 Tss, 1 Tps, 1 inc, 2 Tps (raglan sts), 1 inc; **sleeve:** 1 Tps, *1 Tss, 1 Tps*, rep from * to * to next raglan, 1 inc, 2 Tps (raglan sts), 1 inc; **back:** 1 Tps, *1 Tss, 1 Tps*, rep from * to * to next raglan, 1 inc, 2 Tps (raglan sts), 1 inc; **sleeve:** 1 Tps, *1 Tss, 1 Tps*, rep from * to * to next raglan, 1 inc, 2 Tps (raglan sts), 1 inc; **front:** 1 Tps, 1 Tss, 1 Tps, 1 Tss, 1 Tps.

Work back in return st, work 1 ch. Break off the yarn and pull the end through the ch (100(104:108:108:108:112) sts).

Change to a 7mm (US 10½/11, UK 2) double-ended Tunisian crochet hook and continue in rounds. Place a marker at the start of the round between the 2 raglan sts at the left side of the back. Continue in pattern 2 with raglan increases as follows:

inc 1 st at each side of the front and back on foll 20(22:22:25:28:28) FP and then on foll 2(1:2:1:–:1) alt FP (73(75:79:83:87:91) sts for front and back). **At the same time,** inc 1 st at each side of each sleeve on foll 14(12:12:15:16:16) FP and then on foll 5(6:7:6:6:7) alt FP (55(55:57:61:63:65) sts for each sleeve).

BODY

Then divide the work for the body and sleeves and complete the body first. One of the two raglan sts at each side of the body belongs to the front and the other to the back.

The body consists of 150(154:162:170:178:186) sts, including 2 raglan sts at each side of the front and back.

Make 2 rows of ch to insert in the armholes of the body. Take two lengths of about 16in (40cm) of each yarn for each armhole ch.

Work 9(11:11:11:11:11) ch. Break off the yarn and pull the end through the last ch (8(10:10:10:10:10) ch).

Place a marker at the centre of the ch row to mark the start of the round.

Work 1 round, picking up sts in the back loops of the ch row in each armhole as follows:

Round 1: starting at the marker on the ch row, pick up 4(5:5:5:5:5) sts in the ch row and work in pattern 2 across the front to the second armhole, pick up 8(10:10:10:10:10) sts in the second ch row, work in pattern 2 across the back to the first armhole and pick up the last 4(5:5:5:5:5) sts in the ch row (166(174:182:190:198:206) sts).

Round 2: dec 1 st at each side on the RP (164(172:180:188:196:204) sts).

Continue in rounds in pattern until work measures 20½(20¾:20¾:21¼:21½:21¾) in / 52(52.5:53:54:54.5:55)cm from the centre back neck.

Work 1 round Tps.

Work 2¼in (6cm) in 2 Tss, 2 Tps rib (pattern 1) without shaping.

Bind (cast) off with sl st in rib.

Break off the yarn.

SLEEVES

Start at the centre underarm of the ch row for the body and place a marker here for the start of the round.

Round 1: at each side of the 8(10:10:10:10:10) ch, pick up 2 sts plus the remaining raglan sts. Place markers around all the 3 sts at each side. Work these two sets of 3 sts tog on the RP to prevent holes from forming by the sleeve (65(67:69:73:75:77) sts). Remove all markers except the centre marker.

Continue working in rounds in pattern 2.

Work 2 rounds.

At the next round:

Work 1 FP.

Dec 1 st on each side of marker on the foll RP (63(65:67:71:73:75) sts).

Then dec 1 st on each side of the marker as follows:

dec 1 st at each side on foll 8(9:5:-:-:-) fifth RP, then on foll 3(2:7:13:11:7) fourth RP, and then on foll -(-:-:-:3:8) third RP (41(43:43:45:45:45)sts).

Continue without shaping until sleeve measures 17¼(17¼:17¼:17⅛:17:16½)in / 44(44:44:43.5:43:42)cm from the armhole.

Work 1 round Tps, dec(inc:inc:dec:dec:dec) 1 st at end of RP (40(44:44:44:44:44)sts).

Work 2¼in (6cm) in rounds in 2 Tss, 2 Tps rib and bind (cast) off with sl st in rib (pattern 1).

Break off the yarn.

Make the second sleeve in the same way.

FINISHING

Weave in all ends.

SALVIA

Oversized jacket with pockets

SIZES
US 4(6:8:10:12:14)/UK 8(10:12:14:16:18)

FINISHED MEASUREMENTS
Bust
43¼(46:47¾:49¼:50¾:53½)in /
110(117:121:125:129:136)cm
Length
33¾(34¾:35½:35½:35½:35½)in /
86(88:90:90:90:90)cm

MATERIALS
Yarn
9(10:10:11:12:13–14) balls of Filcolana Tilia
(lace/2-ply) 70% kid mohair, 30% silk in
327 Sage; 1oz/25g/230yd/210m
7(7:7:8:8:9) balls of Filcolana Saga
(light fingering/3-ply) 100% wool in
951 Light Grey; 1¾oz/50g/328yd/300m
Tunisian crochet hook (suggested)
8mm (US 11, UK 0) single-ended with cable
Standard crochet hook
4mm (US 6, UK 8)
Circular knitting needle
4.5mm (US 7, UK 7), 32in (80cm) cable
Stitch markers
Approx. 12
Pins
For finishing sleeves

GAUGE (TENSION)
16 sts x 12 rows (FP and RP) = 4 x 4in
(10 x 10cm) in pattern using one strand of
each yarn and 8mm (US 11, UK 0) Tunisian
crochet hook

SPECIAL TECHNIQUES
End stitch at left edge in 2 vertical bars
(see Techniques, page 138)
Increasing in back vertical bar (see
Techniques, page 152)
Decreasing at both sides on return pass
(see Techniques, page 154)
**Binding (casting) off/decreasing on
forward pass** (see Techniques, page 143)
**Binding (casting) off for shoulder slope,
left side** (see Techniques, page 144)
Italian bind- (cast-) off (see Techniques,
page 170)

PATTERN
Multiple of 6.
FP 1: Tss 1 in each st.
RP 1: work all RP in return st.
FP 2: *3 Tps, 1 Tss, 1 Tps, 1 Tss*, rep from
* to *.
FP 3: as FP 2.
FP 4: *1 Tss, 1 Tps, 1 Tss, 3 Tps*, rep from
* to *.
FP 5: as FP 4.
Rep FP and RP 2–5.

Instructions

The jacket is worked in rows from the bottom up with one strand of each yarn.

FRONT AND BACK

Using one strand of each yarn and an 8mm (US 11, UK 0) Tunisian crochet hook, 171(183:189:195:201:213) ch.

FP 1: start in the second ch from the hook and pick up sts in back loops of the ch row until you have a total of 171(183:189:195:201:213) sts on the hook.
RP 1: work all RP in return st.
Divide the work into fronts and back:

Count 41(44:45:47:48:51) sts in from each side including end st, and place a marker.
FP 2: 1 end st, 1 Tps, 1 Tss, *3 Tps, 1 Tss, 1 Tps, 1 Tss, rep from * to last 5 sts before end st and work 3 Tps, 1 Tss, 1 Tps, 1 end st.
FP 3: as FP 2.
FP 4: 1 end st, 2 Tps, *1 Tss, 1 Tps, 1 Tss, 3 Tps, rep from * to last 5 sts before end st and work 1 Tss, 1 Tps, 1 Tss, 2 Tps, 1 end st.
FP 5: as FP 4.
Rep FP and RP 2–5.
Continue without shaping in pattern until work measures 9½in (24cm).

CHART

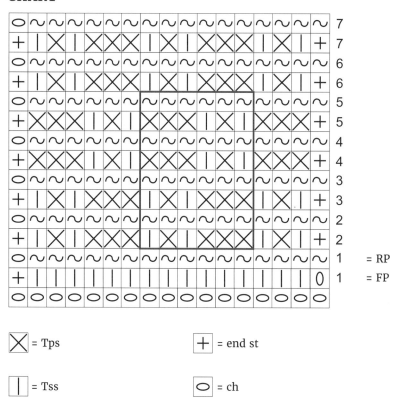

= RP	
= FP	

$\boxed{\times}$ = Tps $\boxed{+}$ = end st

$\boxed{|}$ = Tss $\boxed{\circ}$ = ch

$\boxed{\sim}$ = return st $\boxed{}$ = pattern repeat

Place two more markers, as for the first two at the bottom of the sides for the division between fronts and back. Move these two markers up as the work grows, so you can always check where the fronts and back are divided.

Pockets

Make pockets on each front.

Count 13(14:15:15:16:16) sts from the front edge at each side and place a marker.

Count 23 sts from the first marker and place another marker. These mark the pocket openings.

Complete one pocket first.

Join one strand of each yarn to the 23 sts of the pocket opening and work in rows in pattern, increasing 1 st at each side on the next FP (25 sts).

Continue without shaping until the pocket measures 9½in (24cm), and finish with the same row of the pattern as on the front. Break off the yarn.

Make the second pocket in the same way.

Crochet the pockets to the fronts as follows:

FP 1: work to the last st before the pocket opening, work the last st of the front and the first st of the pocket tog. Work across the rest of the pocket until the last st and work this st and the first st of the back tog. Crochet across the back until the last st before the pocket opening of the second front and crochet the pocket and front tog in the same way as for the first pocket and work to end of row.

Continue without shaping, until work measures 21¾(22¼:22¼:22¼:22:21¾)in / 55(56.5:56.5:56.5:56:55)cm.

Divide the work at the markers and complete the fronts and back separately.

FRONT

Complete the front on the right side of the hook first.

Count 3(4:4:4:4:4) sts from the side marker towards the front edge and place a marker as these will form part of the underarm.

There are 38(40:41:43:44:47) sts remaining on the front.

Work in rows across the front and inc 1 st at the armhole side 2(2:–:2:–:–) times on foll fourth FP, 1 st –(–:1:–:1:1) time(s) on foll ninth FP (40(42:42:45:45:48) sts).

Continue without shaping, until work measures 27½(28:28:28:28:27½)in / 70(71:71:71:71:70)cm.

N.B.: note that you decrease on both FP and RP in the following section.

Bind (cast) off 8(9:5:5:5:5) sts at the neck edge on next 1(1:1:2:1:1) FP, then 4(5:4:4:4:3) sts on foll 1(1:2:1:1:2) FP, and then –(–:2:2:2:2) sts foll –(–:1:1:3:2) FP.

At the same time, dec 1 st at the neck edge on next 3(3:2:2:2:3) RP, and then on foll 1(1:1:–:1:1) alt RP.

At the same time, when work measures 30(30½:32:32:31:31)in / 76.5(77.5:81:81:79:79)cm, bind (cast) off for the shoulder slope as follows:

bind (cast) off 9(9:8:9:9:10) sts at the armhole edge on next two FP (6(6:8:9:9:9) sts).

Work back.

Bind (cast) off with sl st over the remaining sts. Break off the yarn.

Make the second front in the same way, but reversing all shapings.

BACK

Count 3(4:4:4:4:4) sts from the side marker towards the centre back at each side and place a marker as these will form part of the underarm. There are 83(87:91:93:97:103) sts remaining on the back.

Inc 1 st at each side on foll fourth FP 2(2:–:2:–:–) times and then on foll ninth FP –(–:1:–:1:1) times (87(91:93:97:99:105) sts).

Continue without shaping, until work measures 30(30½:32:32:31:31)in / 76.5(77.5:81:81:79:79)cm from centre back neck.

Place a marker on both sides of the central 15(17:19:17:17:19) sts. Work to the first marker, work sl st over the next 15(17:19:17:17:19) sts and work to end of FP. Complete the shoulder on the left side of the hook first. On next FP, bind (cast) off 12(13:13:13:14:14) sts for neck. Continue without shaping until work measures 30(30½:32:32:31:31)in / 76.5(77.5:81:81:79:79)cm. **At the same time** as neck shaping, bind (cast) off for shoulder slope. Bind (cast) off 9(9:8:9:9:10) sts at the armhole edge on next two FP (6(6:8:9:9:9) sts). Work back. Bind (cast) off with sl st over the remaining sts. Break off the yarn. Make the shoulder on the right side of the hook in the same way, but reversing all shapings.

SLEEVES

Using one strand of each yarn and an 8mm (US 11, UK 0) crochet hook, 45(45:45:51:51:51) ch.
FP 1: starting in the second ch from the hook, pick up sts in back loops of the ch row until you have a total of 45(45:45:51:51:51) sts on the hook.
RP 1: work all RP in return st.
Continue in pattern as follows:
FP 2: work 1 end st, 1 Tss, *3 Tps, 1 Tss, 1 Tps, 1 Tss, rep from * to end, 1 end st.
Work one more FP and RP without shaping. On next FP inc 1 st at each side (47(47:47:53:53:53) sts).
Then inc at each side as follows:
inc 1 st at each side on foll −(−:3:−:5:9) third FP, then on foll 8(9:7:5:5:2) fourth FP, then 1(−:−:−:−:−) alt FP, then on foll −(1:1:5:1:1) third FP.

Continue without shaping until work measures 14¼(15:15:15:15:15)in / 36.5(38:38:38:38:38)cm.
N.B.: note that you decrease on both FP and RP in the following section.
Bind (cast) off for top of sleeve at each side as follows:
Sizes US 4, 6 and 8 (UK 8, 10 and 12): bind (cast) off 4 sts on next FP, then 3 sts on foll two FP, **at the same time** dec 1 st on next six RP, then bind (cast) off 3 sts on next FP and 4 sts on foll FP.
Size US 10 (UK 14): bind (cast) off 4 sts on next FP, then 3 sts on foll two FP, **at the same time** dec 1 st on next six RP, then bind (cast) off 2 sts on next FP, then 3 sts on foll FP and then 4 sts on foll FP.
Size US 12 (UK 16): bind (cast) off 4 sts on next FP, then 3 sts on foll FP, **at the same time** dec 2 sts on foll three RP, then dec 1 st on foll RP, then bind (cast) off 3 sts on next FP, and then 4 sts on foll two FP.
Size US 14 (UK 18): bind (cast) off 4 sts on next FP, **at the same time** dec 2 sts on next alt RP, then on foll RP, then dec 1 st on foll two RP, then bind (cast) off 2 sts on foll four FP and then 4 sts on foll two FP.
There are 19(21:23:23:25:25) sts remaining on the hook. Work back.
Bind (cast) off with sl st in pattern over remaining sts, and continue over sts at left side of sleeve top (same principle as Binding (casting) off for shoulder slope, left side, see Techniques, page 144).
Break off the yarn.
Make the second sleeve in the same way.

FINISHING

Weave in the ends.

Change to a 4mm (US 6, UK 8) standard crochet hook and one strand of each yarn. Place the pieces right sides together and crochet the shoulder seams and sleeve seams together with sl st.

Work sl st loosely over the sts at the bottom of both armholes on the body.

Turn the sleeves right side out. Pin the sleeves, right sides together, in the armholes and crochet them in place with sl st with the wrong sides facing you. Crochet the pockets together at each side with sl st. If desired, sew the pocket corners loosely to the front, so the pockets do not flap around.

RIBBING

All the edges of the jacket are knitted in k2, p2 rib with one strand of each yarn on a 4.5mm (US 7, UK 7) circular knitting needle.

Bottom ribbing

On the circular knitting needle, pick up and knit sts in the ch edge with the right side facing you, and **at the same time** inc 1 st in every third ch until you have a total of 228(244:252:260:268:284) sts (1 inc = yo, and work this k tbl or p tbl on the next row).

Work the first inc in the second ch and the last inc in the last ch before the end st. Work 2¾(2¾:2¾:2¾:3¼:3¼)in / 7(7:7:7:8:8)cm in k2, p2 rib, finishing with a wrong side row.

Bind (cast) off with Italian bind- (cast-) off with 2 preparatory rows.

Front border

On the circular knitting needle, pick up and knit sts along the front edges with the right side facing you, and **at the same time** inc 1 st in every alt end st along the rib border at the bottom and evenly spaced along the rest of the front edge until you have a total of 180(184:184:184:190:180) sts.

Work 9 rows in k2, p2 rib, finishing with a wrong side row.

Bind (cast) off with Italian bind- (cast-) off with 2 preparatory rows.

Sleeve cuffs

Work in rounds with circular knitting needle (magic loop) or double-pointed needles.

Pick up and knit 45(45:45:51:51:51) sts in the ch edge with the right side facing you.

Work in rounds in k2, p2 rib, and **at the same time** dec 3(1:1:3:3:3) sts evenly spaced until you have 42(44:44:48:48:48) sts.

Work 2¾(2¾:2¾:2¾:3¼:3¼)in / 7(7:7:7:8:8)cm in rib, finishing with a wrong side row.

Bind (cast) off with Italian bind- (cast-) off with 2 preparatory rows.

COLLAR

With the right side facing you, pick up and knit 122(126:130:130:132:138) sts as follows: Pick up 12 sts in the front ribbing, 28(29:30:30:30:32) sts on the fronts between the front edge and the shoulder seam and 40(42:44:44:46:48) sts along the back.

Row 1: k1 wyif (1 end st), *p2, k2, rep from * to last st, k1.

Row 2: k1 wyif (1 end st), *k2, p2, rep from * to last st, p1.

Rep rows 1 and 2.

N.B.: as the collar will later be folded over with wrong sides facing when sewing up, it is important that any ends from when you change yarn should be on the wrong side of the work.

Work without shaping until the collar measures 15¾in (40cm). Bind (cast) off loosely.

Weave in the ends.

Fold the collar wrong sides together and sew the sides together with mattress st. Then sew the bound- (cast-) off edge to the neck edge with whip st, so the picked up edge will be hidden in the collar.

Weave in the last ends.

Techniques

Foundation row − Each row in Tunisian crochet is made of two parts: the Forward Pass (FP) and the Return Pass (RP). For your foundation row, pick up stitches from a chain and work back across them.

FORWARD PASS (FP)

Pick up loops on the hook in the back loops of the ch row = FP 1.

1. Chain as many stitches as required. (Note that I have used green yarn for the foundation row, and cream yarn for the forward pass at step 3.)

2. Flip the chain stitches over, so the bumps on the back are visible.

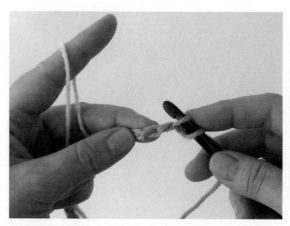

3. Start FP 1 in the second chain from the hook. Insert the hook in the back loop of the chain row.

4. Wrap the yarn around the back of the hook and pull it through so it forms a loop on the hook. There are 2 stitches on the hook, 1 end st and 1 st.

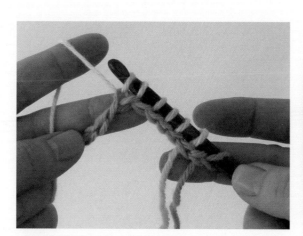

5. Continue picking up stitches on the hook. Note that an attractive, chain-like row is formed under the stitches.

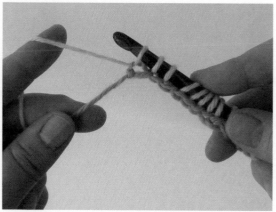

6. Continue picking up stitches until you reach the end of the chain. Now begin your Return Pass to finish the row.

RETURN PASS (RP)

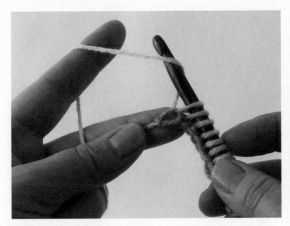

1. **RP 1:** Wrap the yarn around the hook and pull through first loop on hook to form a locking chain.

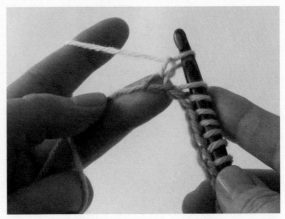

2. This chain makes the end st at the left side.

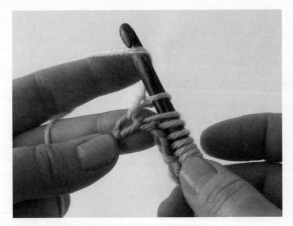

3. Wrap the yarn around the hook from the back.

4. Pull through 2 loops (end st + 1 st). You have now made one stitch.

5. Wrap the yarn around the hook and pull it through the next 2 loops.

6. Repeat until there is 1 loop remaining on the hook. This loop is the first stitch of the next FP and the end st at the right side. FP 1 and RP 1 form the foundation row for all patterns, unless otherwise indicated.

TUNISIAN SIMPLE STITCH (TSS)

1. **FP 2:** Start in the second stitch from the hook. Insert the hook into the front bar. (I have used cream yarn for the FP, and green yarn for Tss.)

2. Wrap the yarn over the hook from the back.

3. Pull it through the bar. There are 2 loops on the hook (1 end st and 1 st).

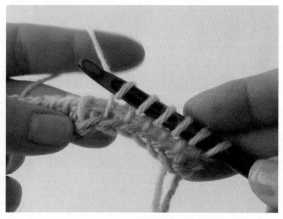

4. Repeat steps 1–3.

5. To work the end st see pages 136–138, then make a Return Pass. All RP are worked as explained on pages 132 and 133.

END STITCH AT LEFT EDGE IN 1 VERTICAL BAR

1. Work to the end st at the left side. (I have used cream yarn for the FP, and green yarn for the end st and for contrast.)

2. Insert the hook in the front loop of the end st.

3. Wrap the yarn around the hook from the back.

4. Pull it through the stitch.

5. Finish the row by making a Return Pass (see pages 132 and 133).

END STITCH AT LEFT EDGE IN 2 VERTICAL BARS

1. Insert the hook in both vertical bars of the end st.

2. Wrap the yarn around the hook from the back.

3. Pull it through both loops and work back as for the Return Pass (see pages 132–133).

TUNISIAN PURL STITCH (TPS)

1. Work the first FP and RP as the foundation row on pages 130–133.

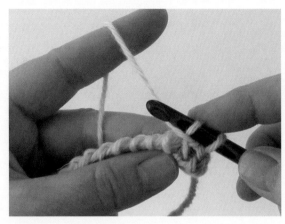

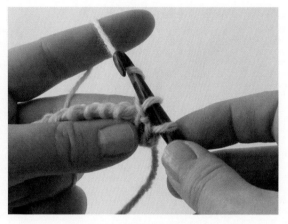

2. With the yarn held in front, insert the hook in the bar of the second stitch from the hook.

3. Wrap the yarn around the hook from the back.

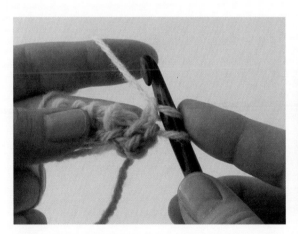

4. Pull it through the loop. There are 2 loops on the hook, 1 end st and 1 Tps.

5. Continue in this way until the last stitch (end st), which is worked in either 1 or 2 vertical bars (see pages 136–138).
Work back as for the Return Pass (see pages 132 and 133).

Here is a piece worked in Tps. The end st at the left side is worked Tks in 1 vertical bar.

BINDING (CASTING) OFF WITH SLIP STITCH IN TUNISIAN SIMPLE STITCH

1. Insert the hook in the next stitch, yarn over and pull through the stitch. There are 2 loops on the hook.

2. Continue to pull the yarn over through the first stitch on the hook. You have worked the first sl st.

3. Continue in this way, working sl st across stitches of the last row.

4. Binding (casting) off with sl st seen from above.

BINDING (CASTING) OFF WITH SLIP STITCH IN TUNISIAN PURL STITCH

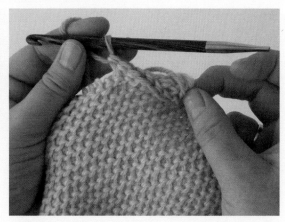

1. Binding (casting) off with sl st in Tps is worked in the same way as for Tss, but holding the yarn in front of your work and making a sl st in each stitch.

2. Binding (casting) off with sl st in Tps seen from above.

BINDING (CASTING) OFF WITH SLIP STITCH IN RIB

Binding (casting) off with slip stitch in rib is worked in the same way as binding (casting) off in Tss and Tps, but working the slip stitch alternately as 1 slip stitch in Tss and 1 slip stitch in Tps.

1. Bind off each stitch in the way that it was previously worked. When you reach a Tss stitch, bind off in Tss.

2. Bind (cast) off the next stitch in Tps.

3. Continue to alternate Tss and Tps bound-(cast-) off stitches until the whole row has been worked, ensuring each stitch is bound off how it was worked.

BINDING (CASTING) OFF/DECREASING ON FORWARD PASS

Bind (cast) off stitches at both edges (here, 5 stitches at each edge).

1. Work sl st over the first 5 sts, continue FP to the last 5 sts of the row and begin your return pass.

2. Continue working across just these stitches (10 stitches bound (cast) off).

BINDING (CASTING) OFF FOR SHOULDER SLOPE, LEFT SIDE

1. Bind (cast) off the neck edge with sl st, then work a forward pass across the shoulder to the stitches that are to be bound off. Finish with a return pass.

2. Repeat this with the next row, working the forward pass to the next lot of stitches to be bound (cast) off, then working the return pass.

3. Using sl st, bind (cast) off the stitches from the last row.

4. Now work into previous rows to create the slope. Use sl st to bind (cast) off the stitches worked in step 1.

5. Now bind (cast) off the stitches that were missed in step 1 with sl st.

6. Once complete, the bind- (cast-) off will have an attractive sloped edge for the shoulder.

BINDING (CASTING) OFF FOR SHOULDER SLOPE, RIGHT SIDE

I have used contrasting yarn for the FP and the sl sts.

1. Bind (cast) off the required number of stitches using sl st. Then make a forward pass on the required number of stitches in the pattern. Work a return pass on these stitches.

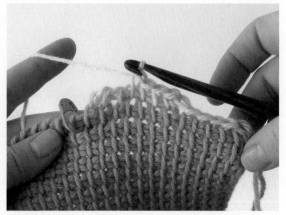

2. Repeat step 1, binding (casting) off the required number of stitches with sl st, then making a forward and return pass on the rest.

3. Bind (cast) off the last shoulder stitches with sl st.

BINDING (CASTING) OFF FOR ARMHOLE WITH SLIP STITCH, BOTH SIDES

1. Bind (cast) off the required number of stitches using sl st, then continue with a forward pass until the next lot of stitches to be bound off. Bind (cast) these off with slip stitch, then break off the yarn and pull the end through the last stitch.

2. Rejoin the yarn on the left edge of the remaining stitches and work the return pass.

3. Continue working in rows over the remaining stitches.

RAGLAN INCREASE IN BACK VERTICAL BAR

The raglan increases start on the second FP.
Place a marker at each side of the 2 raglan stitches.

1. Work to the last st before the raglan stitches.

2. Insert the hook in the back loop of the next stitch.

3. Wrap the yarn over the hook.

4. Pull the yarn over through the st.

5. Insert the hook in the front loop of the same stitch.

6. Yarn over and pull it through the st. You have increased 1 stitch.

7. Work the raglan stitches (here 2 Tps).

8. Insert the hook in the front loop of the next stitch (1 Tks), yarn over, and pull though the stitch.

9. Insert the hook in the back loop.

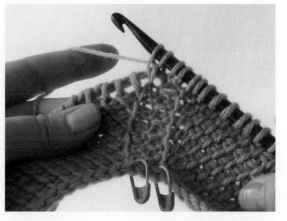

10. Yarn over and pull through the stitch. You have increased 1 stitch.

RAGLAN INCREASE BETWEEN 2 STITCHES

The raglan increases start on the second FP.
Place a marker at each side of the 2 raglan stitches.

1. Work to the 2 raglan sts.

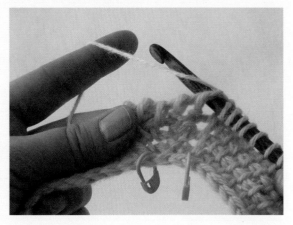

2. Insert the hook in the work between 2 stitches.
Yarn over.

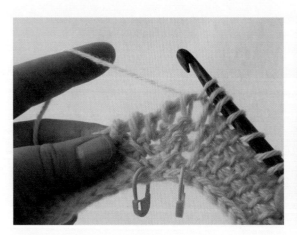

3. Pull the yarn over back through the space. You
have now increased 1 stitch.

4. Work the raglan sts (here 2 Tps).

 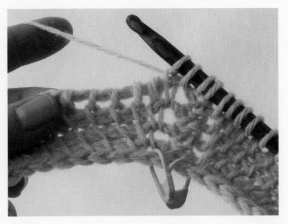

5. Insert the hook in the work between 2 stitches, yarn over and pull the yarn back through the space. You have increased 1 stitch.

6. Work to the end of the forward pass.

INCREASING IN BACK VERTICAL BAR

Increasing on each side of the work (excluding raglan increases).

1. Gently push the stitch towards you so the back bar is visible (see arrow).

2. Insert the hook through the back bar, yarn over.

3. Pull the yarn over through the back bar. You have increased 1 stitch.

4. Work into the front bar of the stitch as normal, then complete the forward pass.

DECREASING AT BOTH SIDES ON RETURN PASS

1. Left side: yarn over and pull through the first st (1 end st).

2. Left side: yarn over and pull it through the return stitch plus 2 stitches (3 loops in total) = 1 stitch decreased.

You can decrease in this way with up to 4 stitches (5 loops in total = 3 stitches decreased). If you need to decrease more stitches, bind (cast) off the stitches (see page 143). However, there may be exceptions, depending on which pattern you are working.

3. Continue to the last 3 stitches of the return pass.

4. Right side: pull the return stitch through 2 stitches together (3 loops in total) = 1 stitch decreased.

5. Pull through the last 2 loops on the hook so that there is only 1 loop left on the hook.

6. Insert the hook in the 2 stitches that were worked together, yarn over.

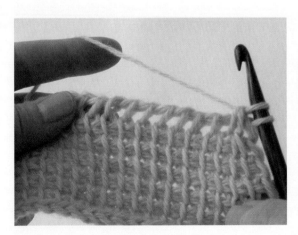

7. Pull the yarn over through both sts.

8. Work to the last 2 stitches that were worked together. Insert the hook in both sts, yarn over and pull though both loops to make the end st.

DOUBLE WHEAT STITCH IN A DIAGONAL LINE

The photo above shows increases and decreases in Tps at each side of the double wheat stitch (dwht).

Increase in Tps to the left of the dwht on the forward pass and decrease in Tps to the right of the wht on the return pass.

The following steps demonstrate working the diagonal double wheat stitch on the left shoulder, when the right side of the work is facing you.

The first FP and RP are worked without decreases and increases.

1. FP 1: work Tss to the last 3 sts, work 1 Tps.

2. Begin the wheat stitch (wht): insert the hook between the next 2 stitches, yarn over.

3. Draw the yarn over back through (1 loop).

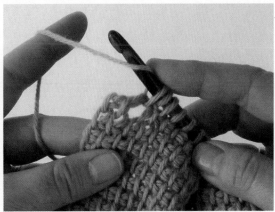

4. Yarn over to form the second loop of the wheat stitch.

5. Insert the hook between the same 2 stitches again and yarn over.

6. Draw the yarn over back through (3 loops on hook). You have made the first half of the wheat stitch.

7. Insert the hook between the last 2 stitches and make the second half of the wheat stitch in the same way (repeat steps 2–6). There are now two groups of 3 loops, a total of 6 loops (1 wht).

8. Work end stitch.

9. RP 1: work end st, then pull through all 6 loops made for the wheat stitch together (1 wht, 7 loops total). Work the rest of the return pass as normal.

10. FP 2: work to the Tps before the wht, work 1 Tps, 1 wht (3 loops on each side of the FP 1 wht).

11. Increase 1 Tps in the back loop of the end st.

12. Work 1 Tss in the front loop of the end st.

13. RP 2: work 1 end st, 1 return st, 1 wht, return 2 stitches together. Work the remainder of the return pass.

14. Steps 10–13 make up the pattern repeat. On the next forward pass, work the R2tog together in Tps.

15. Work 1 wht, increase 1 Tps in back bar of Tps, 1 Tss in front bar of same stitch. Work Tss to end of row.

A left-leaning slant is worked in the same way, increasing to the right of the wht and decreasing to the left.

DOUBLE WHEAT STITCH IN RIB

Multiple of 4 + 3 sts (pattern repeat: *3 Tps, 1 wht*).
See explanation of dwht under Double wheat stitch in a diagonal line (see pages 156–159).

The pattern is worked in rows as follows: 1 end st, 2 Tps, *1 wht, 3 Tps*, rep from * to * to the last 3 sts, and work 2 Tps, 1 end st.

1. Work a foundation row.

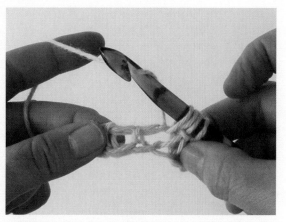

2. FP 2: end st, 1 Tps, work wht as follows: insert the hook in the work between 2 sts, yarn over.

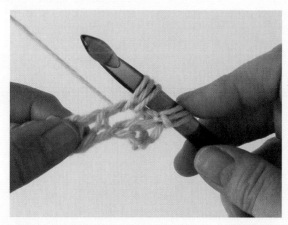

3. Insert the hook in the same space one more time, yarn over and pull the yarn over back through the space (3 loops). You have now made the first half of the wheat stitch.

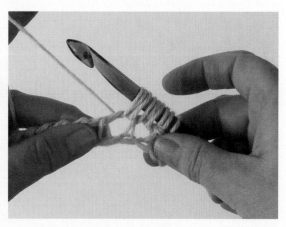

4. Work the second half of the wht in the same way in the next space.

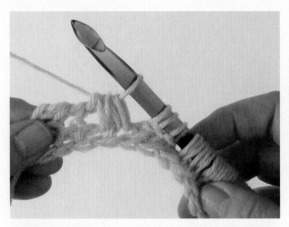

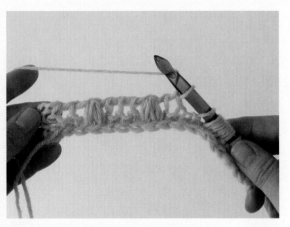

5. On the RP work the 6 loops of the wht together (1 wht).

6. Continue along the row, working each wht together.

7. Repeat steps 2–6 to create wheat stitch rib.

FAUX I-CORD

1. With right side facing, work sl st in the back loops of the stitches where the faux I-cord is required.

WORKING IN ROUNDS

You will need a double-ended hook and two balls of yarn.
Here I chose to work with two different colours.

1. Make a chain row.

2. Join in a ring by picking up a stitch from the back loop of the first chain of the row.

3. First FP of the round: pick up as many stitches as possible in the back loops of the chain row.
This is the right side of the work.

4. First RP of the round: turn so wrong side of the work is facing you. Using the second ball of yarn, work the stitches as for an ordinary return pass.

5. Work back along the round until there are 5 stitches remaining on the hook.

6. Turn work so that the right side of the work is facing you again and continue picking up sts on the hook for the FP.

7. Work forward with the right side out as far as possible.

8. Turn and work back with the wrong side facing you until there are 5 stitches remaining on the hook.
Continue working forward and return passes alternately on the right and wrong side of the work.

CASTING ON NEW STITCHES AT THE ARMHOLE (WHEN WORKING IN ROUNDS)

1. Make 2 rows of chain.

2. Right side: start at the centre of one chain row (start of the round). Pick up stitches on the hook in the back loops of the chain stitches.

3. Continue working across the back to the second armhole.

4. Pick up stitches in the back loops of the second chain row. Continue working across the front to the first armhole and pick up the remaining stitches of the first chain. Place a marker at the start of the round.

MATTRESS STITCH

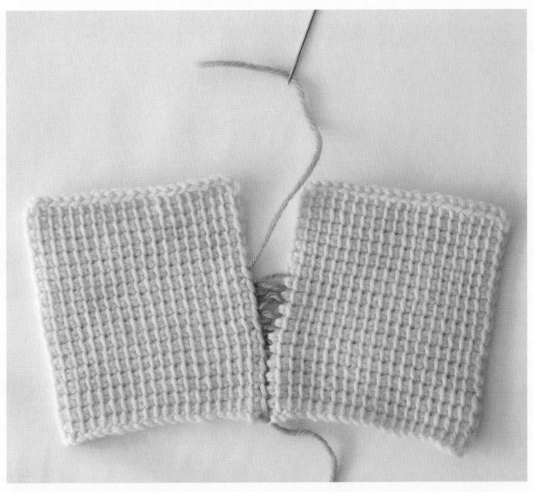

The picture above shows sewing the pieces together with mattress stitch, going back and forth between rows so they are aligned.
Sew the pieces together with the right side facing. If the back sides are being used as the right side, make sure this is facing when sewing.

 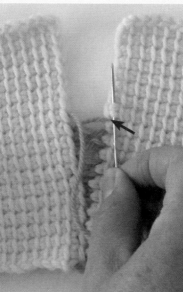 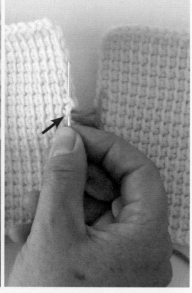

1. Thread a needle with yarn. Place the pieces to be sewn together side-by-side with the right sides facing. Start in the bottom-left corner of the chain edge on the right-hand piece (see dark red arrow). Sew through the chain from the bottom up.

Left-hand piece: Insert the needle from the bottom up through the chain of the cast on edge, then up through one loop of the return stitch (see green arrow) and out again through the end st (see also step 3).

2. Right-hand piece: insert the needle under two horizontal loops (ch) between the end st and the next st.

3. Left-hand piece: insert the needle between the front and back loops of the end st, then through the second loop of the chain in the return pass, on up through the first loop of the chain on the next return pass and out through the front and back loops of the end st. Repeat steps 2 and 3.
Sew a few rows together before pulling the yarn tight.

ITALIAN CAST-ON

For the actual casting on and the first two rows I would recommend that you always use a needle that is one or two sizes (0.5–1mm) smaller than the one you are going to use to knit your work.

Use a length of scrap yarn in a contrasting colour about 39¼in (1m) long and a 4mm (US 6, UK 8) circular knitting needle.
Make a slip knot with the scrap yarn. The scrap yarn will only be used to secure the stitches to the needle until you have worked the first 2 rows.
Cast on the first and last sts with slip knots, so the stitches remain 'locked' on the needle.
Cast on the stitches between as follows: wrap the yarn from the ball round the index finger of your left hand and the scrap yarn around your thumb. *Insert the needle under the scrap yarn and bring the yarn from the ball up on to the needle, insert the needle back around the yarn from the ball and over the needle, rep from * until you have the desired number of sts minus 1, which you make when casting on with a slip knot.

N.B.: before making the last stitch with the slip knot, wind the scrap yarn and the knitting yarn around each other once. Work the next 2 rows as described below. Do not knit the scrap yarn in with them. Turn the work. Work in rows.
Row 1: p1, *k1, p1 wyif*, rep from * to last st, p1. Remove the loop of scrap yarn from the needle.
Row 2: sl1, *k1, p1 wyif, rep from * to last stitch, k1.
Change to a 5mm (US 8, UK 6) circular knitting needle.
Rep rows 1 and 2 once more, making a total of 4 rows.

ITALIAN BIND- (CAST-) OFF

For Italian bind- (cast-) off, work 2 or 4 preparatory rounds after your ribbing in k1, p1 as follows:

Round 1: work *k1, p1 wyif, rep from * to end of round.

Round 2: work *k1 wyif, p1, rep from * to end of round (2 preparatory rounds).

Rep rounds 1 and 2 once more (4 preparatory rounds).

Do not break the yarn. Measure the length of the edge to be bound (cast) off and use an end of yarn three times that length for sewing. Thread a yarn needle. Place a marker in the first knit stitch and the following purl stitch. You have to sew through each stitch (both k and p), as if grafting two pieces together.

Start by securing the first knit stitch. Insert the needle purlwise into the knit stitch and pull the yarn through. Insert the needle from the back between the first knit stitch and the next purl stitch and pull the yarn all the way through. Insert the needle knitwise from the front in the purl stitch and insert the needle knitwise from the front in the knit stitch and slip it off the knitting needle. Miss the purl stitch and insert the needle purlwise in the next knit stitch. *Go back to the first purl stitch, insert the needle purlwise in the stitch and slip it off the knitting needle. Miss the knit stitch and insert the needle from the back between the knit stitch and the next purl stitch and knitwise in the purl stitch.

Go back to the knit stitch, insert the needle knitwise in the knit stitch and slip it off the knitting needle. Miss the purl stitch and insert the needle purlwise in the next knit stitch. Rep from * to end of round. Finish the round by sewing through the 2 marked sts, so they are fastened off.

N.B.: when the yarn is at the front of the work you will sew the purl stitch and when the yarn is at the back of the work you will sew the knit stitch. That way you will never be in doubt about what to do next after taking a break.

Yarns

FILCOLANA
Alva (lace/2-ply) 100% alpaca;
1oz/25g/192yd/175m

Anina (fingering/4-ply) 100% superwash
merino wool; 1¾oz/50g/230yd/210m

Arwetta Classic (fingering/4-ply)
80% superwash merino wool, 20% nylon;
1¾oz/50g/230yd/210m

Merci (fingering/4-ply) 50%
superwash wool, 50% pima cotton;
1¾oz/50g/219yd/200m

Pernilla (light fingering/3-ply),
100% Peruvian highland wool;
1¾oz/50g/192yd/175m

Tilia (lace/2-ply) 70% kid mohair,
30% silk; 1oz/25g/230yd/210m

ISAGER YARN
Alpaca 1 (lace/2-ply) 100% alpaca;
1¾oz/50g/438yd/400m

Highland wool (light fingering/3-ply)
100% wool; 1¾oz/50g/301yd/275m

Silk Mohair (lace/2-ply) 75% kid mohair,
25% silk; 1oz/25g/232yd/212m

CARL J. PERMIN
Elise (fingering/4-ply) 90% cotton,
10% cashmere; 1oz/25g/126yd/115m

GO HANDMADE
Tencel Bamboo Fine (fingering/
4-ply) 40% tencel, 60% bamboo;
1¾oz/50g/230yd/210m

VILLY JENSEN
Lammy Lurex (fingering/4-ply)
100% polyester; 1¾oz/50g/175yd/160m

KREMKE SOUL WOOL
Stellaris (lace/2-ply) 47% viscose,
41% polyester, 12% metallic yarn;
1oz/25g/613yd/560m

KREA DELUXE
Shiny (fingering/4-ply) 80% viscose,
20% polyester; 1oz/25g/104yd/95m

Accessories

STITCH MARKERS

I use a great many stitch markers in my work.
I place markers at every decrease and increase and
also at the neck edge, armhole and raglan stitches.
For me, this works as a check, because it is
immediately obvious if I have forgotten a decrease
or an increase.

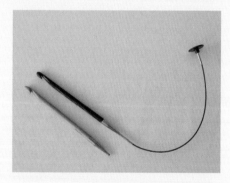

SINGLE-ENDED CROCHET HOOK
WITH CABLE

These hooks are essential for working to and fro in
rows. The hooks are also available in plastic.

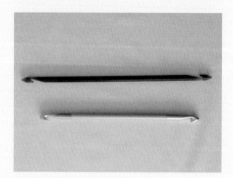

DOUBLE-ENDED CROCHET HOOKS

These hooks are essential for working in rounds.
Double-ended crochet hooks are also available in
bamboo and wood.

Finishing techniques

Tunisian crochet garments may have a tendency to pull out of shape during making. Blocking the garments once complete is therefore recommended. I often just steam the finished piece very carefully, unless it needs to be washed. If you choose to wash your work, always check the instructions on the ball band.

STEAM BLOCKING

Using a steam iron, set the iron to full steam.
NEVER place the iron directly on your work; hold it ½in (1cm) above it, moving the iron around gently above your work. Put the iron down while carefully patting and pulling the work into shape.

TRADITIONAL WET BLOCKING

Gather a bowl, wool wash detergent and warm water at 86 degrees fahrenheit (30 degrees celsius).
Dissolve the detergent in the water and soak the work in it for a moment. Take it out and squeeze out the water.
Rinse the work three times, squeezing the water out after every rinse.
Lay the work flat between two towels, shaping it as required.
Roll the towels up into a sausage shape and wring them.
Unroll the towels. Take a dry towel and shape the work on it, letting it dry flat.

WET BLOCKING IN ONE BATCH OF WATER

There are several no rinse wool detergents available, which do not have to be washed out after soaking. The one I use is called Eucalan.
Gather a bowl, wool wash detergent and warm water at 86 degrees fahrenheit (30 degrees celsius).
Dissolve the detergent in the water and soak the work in it for a moment. Take it out and squeeze out the water.
Lay the work flat between two towels, shaping it as required.
Roll the towels up into a sausage shape and wring them.
Unroll the towels. Take a dry towel and shape the work on it, letting it dry flat.

MACHINE WASH

There are big differences in how gently machines wash woollen garments.
I would not recommend washing mohair in a washing machine.
Use liquid wool wash and set the washing machine to the wool setting.
N.B.: before you wash your work in the washing machine, I recommend you wash your swatch to avoid getting a nasty surprise.
When the work has been washed, lay it flat to dry in the desired shape.

Acknowledgements

In a very turbulent period when the global pandemic was turning everything and everyone upside down, we became more acutely aware that things do not always happen as a matter of course. The importance of all kinds of crafts and being together with other people acquired a whole new meaning.

And in my case, having the opportunity to write this book filled me with deep gratitude and affection for all you wonderful people who helped to make it possible for my grand dream to come true.

ORIGINAL PUBLISHER
Many thanks to Forlaget Turbine and in particular to Marie Brocks Larsen, publishing director and partner, for your fantastic collaboration and your belief in my idea. Marie, thank you for agreeing that Oliver Rosendal should take the photos for the book and for your professional oversight throughout.

LAYOUT
Many thanks to graphic designer, Karin Hald, for the amazingly beautiful layout of the book.

EDITOR
Many thanks to the editor Rachel Søgaard for her technically well-informed and professional editing of all the patterns – and for inspiring discussions.

YARN COMPANIES
A big thank you to Filcolana, Isager Yarn, Permin and Go Handmade for their great collaboration and for providing the yarns for my designs. Thank you for trusting me and my abilities. I am very much looking forward to being able to show you the finished designs in this book.

PHOTOGRAPHER
Oliver Rosendal / VINIA Media
Many thanks, Oliver, for an absolutely magical and super professional photoshoot. You have a unique and very engaging way of getting people to relax in front of the camera. I am so pleased that it was you who took the photos for the book.

RETOUCHING
Mathias Vilhelmsen / VINIA Media
Thank you for retouching the photos for the book.

HAIR AND MAKE-UP ARTIST
Many thanks to Emilie Preskou for styling all my lovely friends who wore my designs during the photoshoot. You have a wonderful talent for creating something natural and beautiful. Being styled by you was a great experience in every way.

MY WONDERFUL FAMILY

A huge loving thank you to my husband, Jan Mathorne, my daughter, Therese Kampp Mathorne, and my son, Patrick Kampp Mathorne. Without your invaluable support and help and your confidence in my ability to 'climb my mountain', this would not have been possible. I love you!

CROCHETING THE DESIGNS

A big thank you to Therese Kampp Mathorne and Laila Binder for your help.

MODELS IN THE BOOK

Many thanks to Therese Kampp Mathorne, Jenny Færch, Karin Højgaard Jeppesen, Louise Suhr Mertins and Paula Vest for agreeing to wear my designs for the book. Having you as my models brought my ideas for the book together.

You helped to create an absolutely magical photoshoot!

When all the photos for the patterns were in place, you began to have fun. You took turns wearing the various tops, sweaters and jackets and, even if the sizes weren't specifically designed for you, the result was a magical space, full of new possibilities.

About the author

Is there anything better than being busy with something that is both your job and your hobby? For me, having yarn between my fingers is a lifestyle I cannot be without.

I always have several projects on the go. An undemanding one for when I want to be sociable or need to relax, a more technical project and another in which I investigate new techniques and yarns.

All my life I have busied myself with handicrafts. I trained as a craft teacher at Hellerup Håndarbejdsseminarium (Hellerup Crafts College in Denmark) and I have taught and held workshops on both sewing and yarn in various capacities.

In addition, for years, I created designs for Burda International Nordic for the magazines Alt om Håndarbejde (*All About Crafts*) and Kreativ Strik (*Creative Knitting*).